Covenant with God: God's Relationship With Man

Chris A. Legebow

DEDICATION

I thank God for the teachers and preachers in my early Christian years who
have made me to understand the covenants of God. I thank God for
Christian Broadcasting especially Trinity Broadcasting Network.
I thank Kenneth and Gloria Copeland, Benny Hinn, Marilyn Hickey and
Joyce Meyer for their excellent teachings that have strengthened me.

CONTENTS

ACKNOWLEDGMENTS

All Scripture taken from Biblegateway.com
Most Scripture taken from Modern English Version (MEV)
Some scripture taken from King James Version (KJV)

INTRODUCTION

If you are reading this book, you must have a sincere desire to learn more about God and His promises to people throughout the history of the earth. God's promises are more than mere words. He cannot lie and therefore what He promises He surely will do. We were created to have relationship with God. Humans are designed to want to know about spiritual things. We are fascinated by the spiritual or supernatural; it is because we were meant to be communing with God. God created us so that we could talk with Him, live with Him and worship Him.

In God's presence is joy, peace, eternal unconditional love. Why our relationship with God is the most important relationship we could have is because as we receive Jesus Christ as our Saviour, He comes to live on the inside of our human spirit. God living in us is the most intimate, dynamic and inspiring relationship possible.

God's love for humans is so strong that even though throughout history man has broken the covenants or promises of God, by not fulfilling man's part of the contract, God has made new covenants with different people. A covenant is a two-part agreement to something. God has constantly made new ways of connecting with us by searching for righteous people to whom He could communicate His truths. The Bible is a record of God's dealings with man. It also clearly shows the ways for man to live pleasing to God.

Many people don't like to think of giving their lives to serve God. They would consider it a punishment, as if they were losing something as though living for God would make them less themselves. It is the exact opposite. Only through right relationship with God can man know freedom. God did not create us to be as robots who would obey without choice. The special part of our relationship with God is we choose it. God will never force Himself on any one. God gave us free will, the freedom of choice.

By His mercy towards us, He draws us to Himself. Usually, someone starts praying for you and in the angelic realm, angels are surrounding you making it possible for you to consider God and desiring to know about Him. There are so many false gods and so many religions, it might seem hard to decide what to choose. The deception is that there is more than one God. There is only one true God – the God who created all things. He revealed Himself to different people in different ways but He is the "I AM." That means He was God; He is God; He will always be God.

God's love towards us is so strong that He continually kept revealing Himself to individuals as detailed in the Bible so that we might come to truly know Him and believe in Him. The study of the Covenants of God begins with Adam and Eve who were given dominion over all the creatures of the earth and the earth itself. They had freedom to obey God or not obey God. There was only one requirement to their covenant; they were not to eat of the tree of the knowledge of good and evil. They could have any other thing they wanted in the Garden of Eden. Because they sinned, they willfully disobeyed God – God promised that an end to the original sin that would be born into every child because of their sin, would be ended by the coming of a Messiah. The shedding of an animal's blood as sacrifice began. It was as the product, "white out" that covers a place when typing with a typewriter and you want to cover an error; you dab the liquid white out and the error is covered. It doesn't not remove the sin; it simply covers it until the Messiah would come.

God's dealings with Noah were special. There were only eight people who were spared from God's judgement on the earth in the early history of earth. It was Noah and his family. God's promise to Noah was that his life would be saved, and his family, if he would build a huge boat, an ark that would hold him and many animals. He preached warning the people around him of the coming danger, but they only mocked him, so none of them were saved. Noah and his family would repopulate the earth after a terrible worldwide flooding that destroyed all other people and all other animals. God promised that never again would such a thing happen to man or animals and made a promise that He gave us a rainbow in the sky as a sign of this promise.

Abraham was a special man who wanted to know God even though he lived among idol worshippers. He wanted to know the one true God and God revealed Himself to Abraham by getting him to leave his family and all that he knew to travel to a land that God would lead Him to. It was a total commitment of faith that caused Abraham to obey God. He didn't know where he was going, only that he knew he had heard God speaking to him. As he followed, God promised Abraham that from him would come mighty kings of the earth, the origin of many nations, with a lineage too long to count even as the sands on a beach or the stars in the sky in number. Through a miraculous birth of their son Isaac who came as they were in their 90's, Abraham's legacy began.

Moses was a promised deliverer of Israel, the seed of Abraham who became slaves in Egypt. Moses obeyed God almost perfectly. He experienced miracles and spoke God's word with the help of his brother Aaron to the Pharaoh of Egypt. There were plagues as judgments on Egypt each occasion that Pharaoh denied freedom of the Israelites. After the death of the first born children in Egypt, there was much sorrow and finally Pharaoh let Israel go free. Moses brought the children of Israel to Mount Sinai where he was given the commandments of God. Moses lead the people of Israel for 40 years through the wilderness because Israel kept disobeying Jehovah (I AM).

Animal blood sacrifice was officiated by the tribe of Levi. They were consecrated as holy people to serve God all their lives and in all the generations to come. Moses had been give the pattern to build a Tabernacle in the wilderness – a place where God's presence would be with the people. The glory of God would fill the tabernacle. The glory of God would rest upon it as a bright light. Moses had a long relationship with God and would speak with God directly.

Israel entered into the promised land and knew prosperity peace and blessing because of King David. King David was special in that he loved God and honoured him and celebrated his presence. David wanted to build a Temple for God but because he was a warrior and shed much blood, God gave his son Solomon the project of building a temple to God. God promised David that through his lineage would come the Messiah.

Many evil kings led Israel into pagan idol worship. Prophets spoke to Israel warning them that if they did not repent, God would remove them from their promised land and that they would lose Israel including the temple of God where God's presence was residing. After the destruction of Jerusalem and the temple, animal sacrifice was no longer practiced because there was no temple. Israel was scattered and taken captive by enemies. Prophecies remained that Israel would be rebuilt and that Messiah would come and bring reconciliation of Israel to God. Hope of relationship with God still existed.

Finally, after 400 years of silence from God with no prophets proclaiming news, Jesus was born. He fulfilled many Messianic prophecies proving that he was the Son of God. His birth and all aspects surrounding it was filled with prophecy, angels and faithful people who loved God. He lived an ordinary life until he was 30 years old. It was then that he began his earthly ministry preaching that he was the Messiah who had come to free Israel from her sins. Israel existed. The temple had been rebuilt, but Israel was captive by Rome. Jesus preached and demonstrated the authority of

God on the earth with miracles, healings and even the resurrection from the dead. Jesus gathered followers and for three years he impacted the earth with preaching, teaching, miracles, signs and wonders. All people ran from him when he was arrested and tried for blasphemy because he said he was the Son of God. Jesus gave his life as a sacrifice so that whosoever would believe on his death, burial and resurrection would be saved from their sins.

Jesus lived a holy life keeping all the commandments and he offered his holy life as a sacrifice for those who would believe in Him. Jesus not only restored the relationship of man with God but also paid the penalty for sin so that the presence of God could come and dwell inside of believers. Jesus brought the hope that we could living pleasing to God by giving us the person of the Holy Spirit, the comforter, the teacher and the seal of God's promise. Christians believe He will return to the earth and rule and reign and we will be with Him for eternity. The New Covenant erases sin, the desire for sin and the penalty for sin. By confessing our sins to God and believing in Jesus Christ we are made holy – one with God. By God's indwelling presence and our giving of ourselves to God as a living sacrifice each day, we live in the Spirit and choose God and His ways rather than any other way. Jesus saves; Jesus heals; Jesus delivers. The New Covenant is the fulfillment of God's promise to Adam and Eve that Messiah would come. It fulfills the promise to Noah that God would not always strive with man but there would come a strong relationship between us. The New Covenant fulfills the promise to Abraham in that we who believe in Jesus Christ are made heirs of Abraham by faith. We are of that multitude of descendants promised who would serve and honour God.

Jesus blood shed for us fulfilled the requirement of the laws of Moses that demanded an animal sacrifice for sin. Jesus blood was offered once for all eternity that whoever believes in the blood of Jesus, would be forgiven. His blood erases the sins as though they never existed. Jesus keeping all the commandments given to Moses, is our Saviour who seals the promises of God made to Israel. The Gentiles have been grafted into the tree of life through Jesus Christ. Jew and Gentile are united in the Messiah Jesus. God's promise to us is that He will return and rule and reign on the earth and we will be with Him.

Knowing the covenants of God helps us to understand different aspects of God as He revealed His glory to us throughout the history of the Bible. It is my prayer that you will enjoy the study of God's covenants with man, His desire to establish permanent relationship with humans.

1. ADAMIC COVENANT

Adamic Covenant – God's Covenant with Adam and Eve

Covenant

Covenant isn't a word we use very much in our North American society. It is a word that means more than a promise. It is a promise you would keep even if it costs you your life. The word is still used in the modern Christian Church but not all people understand its meaning. In the Biblical definition, a covenant is an agreement that you make with someone where you pledge to help that person as long as you live or die in the attempt to help that person if the person requires help. It is like a contract because it is most certainly official. For an in depth teaching on the meaning of the Blood Covenant of Jesus, I would highly recommend Kenneth Copeland's multi – cd teaching on the Blood Covenant.

Eastern people, I mean the Eastern world such as Israel and ancient Eastern countries, thought of covenant most seriously. Some of these cultures still do regard it as a promise that you would pledge your life to keep. The agreement was literally sealed with the participant's blood. When making a covenant, one person, usually of some wealth and power would agree with a different leader, of some wealth or power, would agree to their mutual benefit. It would be similar to a peace treaty but much more potent. The people would swear to protect the other person and their agreement towards that person and his tribe or die trying to do so. It meant there was no place for loopholes. It was totally unlike any modern agreement. The culmination of this covenant would mean that the main leaders would cut their own arms so blood would come. Both of them, would put their bleeding arms together and sometimes it was wrapped while they swore to protect each other. The blood represented the willingness to die to keep the covenant.

Covenant relationship meant caring for one another and trade and economic friendship. It also meant they could marry amongst their tribes. Middle East nations still have this view of covenant. If someone were to fight against one of the covenant tribes, the other person and all his tribe would fight as though it was their enemy also. It was a way of organizing societies to maintain peace and strengthen the tribes, but it cannot be confirmed as being serious without the shedding of blood of the leaders. If the person were to break the covenant it would cost the person his or her life.

In North America, you will most normally hear of it as the marriage covenant. God's idea of marriage is that much of a promise – literally until death do us part is what God intended it to be. I believe that in the last 50 or 60 years, the meaning of marriage has completely been changed. People get divorced for all sorts of reasons including not loving the person any more or because there is someone else or because he or she wants more freedom in life. None of these would have been acceptable reasons for divorce. Moses, the person God gave the commandments to, only permitted divorce because of the hardness of men's hearts (Matthew 19: 8). God's word clearly indicates that God hates divorce (Malachi 2: 16). God created man (men and women) to live in covenant relationships.

If we taught marriage as it is suppose to be, perhaps less people would marry, or perhaps more people would never divorce. Please know that there are valid reasons for people to separate. In no way is this message meant to condemn those who are divorced. If there is abuse of any kind or unfaithfulness of a spouse, there are reasons to separate. What this teaching is emphasizing is God's view of what covenant should be. Native aboriginal peoples have a type of treaty that is similar to covenant in the sense that I am speaking of. It is an oath or vow that you keep with all your being.

Covenants made by God are different than covenants made by people. The only one who can break covenant is the human, God never breaks His covenants. He makes covenant and swears by Himself – and it is impossible for Him to lie or go against Himself. It is God's promise to us. The Adamic covenant is the first covenant made with people because God created Adam and Eve and made covenant with them.

Most people refer to the Old Testament as the Old Covenant. What they usually refer to is the covenant God made with Moses. The New Testament is usually referred to as the New Covenant which is God's promises to all who are Christians that believe on Jesus Christ's death, burial, resurrection and the promise of His coming again. There are several covenants that God has made with people. We will study them in other chapters: Adamic, Abrahamic, Noahtic, Mosaic, and The New Covenant.

The Adamic Covenant

The Adamic Covenant is an agreement God made with Adam. God created Adam and Eve as it states in Genesis 1. God placed Adam and Eve in a beautiful lush garden called Eden. They could have anything they wanted in that garden. There were many fruit bearing trees and bushes. They could have had any of it except for the one tree – Adam was told not to eat of it. Please realize the place was abounding with every kind of delicious fruit a person could want. Adam and Eve were told to tend it – which mostly meant picking fruit because there were no thorns or thistles or bugs or any negative thing. The animals were named by Adam. There was no killing or bloodshed. The animals lived in harmony with mankind. Adam and Eve were given dominion over all the earth.

Dominion is a word that we hardly hear anymore. It means responsibility and authority. Most Christians understand the word stewardship which means the care of a sphere of influence with rights and responsibilities and authority. Adam and Eve were given authority over all creatures of the earth: fish, birds, reptiles, mammals, all creatures. The tree of life was present in that garden. Many interpret the tree of life to be Jesus Christ. If they had taken fruit of the tree of life they would have lived forever as Holy people. They were given freedom in all parts of their lives and concerning all the earth except – the tree of the knowledge of good and evil. They were not to eat of that tree.

Genesis 3: 2 And the woman said to the serpent, "We may eat of the fruit from the trees of the garden; 3 but from the fruit of the tree which is in the midst of the garden, God has said, 'You will not eat of it, nor will you touch it, or else you will die.' "

Many people wonder why God would put the tree of the knowledge of Good and Evil in the garden at all. The truth was this – God wants us to freely choose Him and His will for us. He gave us a most precious gift – free will. That means we do not have to obey God or serve Him if we do not want to. Free will means that is possible for us to choose a different way than God's way. Please see true worship is not because someone is forcing you to do it. It is an act of human will - saying – Yes, I want to worship you God with all that is within me. God did not want us to be a people who serve Him because we don't have any other choice. Many people have difficulty accepting God because they don't want to stop being their own god. These people do anything they want, and answer to no one. They in fact are in enmity or at war with God. They strongly will to disobey God. The human soul is the mind, will and emotions of a person. A person who will not submit to God is foolish because there is no way people could have a life superior to what God could and would give them.

Adam and Eve knew life in its most glorious aspect. They walked and talked with God. God let Adam name all the creatures. God was sharing His heart with Adam and Eve. They were in a heaven like existence knowing only good and holiness.

The Tree of Knowledge of Good and Evil

God never created us to know evil. God created us in His image and likeness. That means we were living in a pure, Holy condition before sin. Some secular historians refer to this period as Innocence. Unfortunately, with that term of Innocence comes the connotation of ignorance and that is simply not true. Adam and Eve only knew good. They knew how to explore the garden. They loved each other. They talked intimately with God each day. They were naked but unashamed (Genesis 2: 25). I believe they had a covering of glory on them. They were created in God's image and God is light. God shines with radiance and brilliance. Adam and Eve would have been pure and without sin and without a carnal mind so they would have seen each other with only pure and holy love for one another.

Some people interpret the tree of the knowledge of Good and evil to be partaking of sex but that is ridiculous. God created sex. He meant there to be pleasure in the love between a man and woman. He wanted them to have joy in each other and in their family. The tree of the knowledge of Good and evil was as its name says – it is knowing evil. Mankind was never meant to know evil. Evil is anything contrary to God and it always leads to death and destruction.

The Serpent Tempted and Seduced Eve

Genesis 3: 4 Then the serpent said to the woman, "You surely will not die! 5 For God knows that on the day you eat of it your eyes will be opened and you will be like God, knowing good and evil."

It is most certain that Adam and Eve spoke with and to the animals because the woman was not surprised by a serpent speaking to her. Satan possessed a serpent. It is uncertain what the creature resembled but it was beautiful. It had legs like a dragon because part of the curse upon it was it losing its legs. The serpent appealed to Eve's free will – the root of the statement was to cause her to doubt God's goodness and God's provision to her. He promises her that her disobedience will not lead to death but that she would be as a god. Adam was with her and yet he said nothing. He also was tempted to disobey God.

Genesis 3: 6 When the woman saw that the tree was good for food, that it was pleasing to the eyes and a tree desirable to make one wise, she took of its fruit and ate; and she gave to her husband with her, and he ate. 7 Then the eyes of both were opened, and they knew that they were naked. So they sewed fig leaves together and made coverings for themselves.

1 John 2: 16 16 For all that is in the world—the lust of the flesh, the lust of the eyes, and the pride of life—is not of the Father, but is of the world.

Please notice Eve focused on the forbidden fruit. It seemed to be most beautiful. She desired it even though it was forbidden. She lusted after it. She thought within herself that she could be like God - this pride compelled her to partake of the fruit of the tree of the knowledge of good and evil and her husband Adam took of it too because he was there with her.

Sin Enters Humans

Adam did not keep the garden. He should have taken authority over that serpent and rebuked it for lying about God. He did not. He should have spoken to his wife to believe God not a serpent. They should have cried out to God to intervene. I believe He would have manifest Himself to them. The truth was, both Adam and Eve disobeyed God. It was a sin against God's covenant with them. Immediately they knew they were naked. I believe that what died was not only their innocent state but the glory that was on them was no longer there because they had broken their covenant with God. They had lost their anointing covering of God's presence.

There was a consequence for their sin. Something died that moment. It was their close relationship with God. Adam and Eve were ashamed of their nakedness and sewed leaves together to cover themselves. From who? They only had each other but shame is a consequence of sin. They were not created to know shame. They also grew afraid of God. Fear entered the world because of sin. They were not created to know fear.

Genesis 3: 8 Then they heard the sound of the Lord God walking in the garden in the cool of the day, and the man and his wife hid themselves from the presence of the Lord God among the trees of the garden. 9 The Lord God called to the man and said to him, "Where are you?"

10 He said, "I heard Your voice in the garden and was afraid because I was

naked, so I hid myself."

Once they are caught, rather than repent or ask for forgiveness they play a blame game. Adam blames Eve for getting him to sin. Eve blames the serpent. Indirectly they both blame God. They do not realize what they have done is wrong. Part of the consequence of sin is getting a hard heart to God.

Genesis 3: 11 And He said, "Who told you that you were naked? Have you eaten from the tree of which I commanded you not to eat?"

12 The man said, "The woman whom You gave to be with me, she gave me fruit of the tree, and I ate."

13 Then the Lord God said to the woman, "What have you done?"

And the woman said, "The serpent deceived me, and I ate."

God judges the sins of the serpent. I must believe that the serpent was willing to let Satan use him. God would not judge this animal unless the animal had in some way been a part of the sin.God's judgement is harsh upon the serpent.

The Judgement on both the Serpent (Animal) and on Satan who Possessed it.

Genesis 3: 14 The Lord God said to the serpent: "Because you have done this,

You are cursed above all livestock,
    and above every beast of the field;
you will go on your belly,
    and you will eat dust
    all the days of your life.
15 I will put enmity
    between you and the woman,
    and between your offspring and her offspring;
he will bruise your head,
    and you will bruise his heel."

The reference in verse 15 is very special because it proclaims that an offspring of the woman will " bruise its head" this signifying the coming of Jesus Christ as Saviour.

The Judgement on the Woman

The woman had severe consequences also because of her sin. I believe she would have been able to have children with no pain or suffering. She was created as an equal with man but the consequence of sin made her subject to him. [I thank God for Jesus and the Covenant who made of us equals once more!]

Genesis 3: 16 To the woman He said,

"I will greatly multiply your pain in childbirth,
    and in pain you will bring forth children;
your desire will be for your husband,
    and he will rule over you."

The Judgement on the Man

The consequences to Adam are perhaps the most severe. God had created Adam first so it makes sense that Adam should have known God more and not sinned.

Genesis 3: 17 And to Adam He said, "Because you have listened to the voice of your wife and have eaten from the tree about which I commanded you, saying, 'You shall not eat of it,'

Cursed is the ground on account of you;
    in hard labor you will eat of it
    all the days of your life.
18 Thorns and thistles it will bring forth for you,
    and you will eat the plants of the field.
19 By the sweat of your face
    you will eat bread
until you return to the ground,
    because out of it you were taken;
for you are dust,
    and to dust you will return."

Because of Adam's sin, the earth and all the realms of the universe were cursed. Because of it, animals no longer had the same relationship with people or with each other. They became carnivores. Man would have to work hard to grow his fruit and food. The ground was cursed to have thorns and thistles and weeds. Work would be difficult. Rather than simply pick the fruit, he had to dig the soil and plant and work to make it grow. Also, death entered into the human race. If Adam and Eve had never sinned, they would never have died. Because of their sin, God gave people a life span.

Even though they had sinned, God did not destroy them and start all over. He provided a solution. The first animal sacrifice of blood occurred.

Genesis 3: 21 The Lord God made garments of skins for both Adam and his wife and clothed them. 22 The Lord God said, "The man has become like one of us, knowing good and evil. And now, he might reach out his hand, and take also from the tree of life, and eat, and live forever"— 23 therefore the Lord God sent him out from the garden of Eden, to till the ground from which he was taken. 24 He drove the man out, and at the east of the garden of Eden He placed the cherubim and a flaming sword which turned in every direction, to guard the way to the tree of life.

Animal Skins

God replaced their fig leaves with animal skins. Although the scripture does not specifically say that an animal sacrifice was given as atonement, all further references to animal sacrifice as atonement for sin is mentioned. The skins of the animals would have represented both their need for natural covering and their need for spiritual covering (of an animal's blood). If Adam and Eve would have eaten from the tree of life (eternal life) in their sinful state, they would have never been able to receive redemption. They would have lived in sin without hope of reconciliation to God. God made them leave the garden of Eden that had been the only home they knew and set up an angel to guard the way so no one could reenter.

What this Means to Humans

For thousands of years, people hoped for the offspring of the woman that would crush the serpent's head. Even in all the other covenants we discuss, they all speak of the Messiah who would come to restore man and God. God didn't give up on people. He had a plan to redeem us and give us intimate relationship with God once more. The hope is in the Saviour, the LORD Jesus Christ.

Inherited Sin – Original Sin

What it meant for all humans is the tendency to sin. It is an iniquity or inherited sin because we are the descendants of Adam and Eve. All people on earth are born in sin. The most beautiful babies have a trace of original sin. That means we must have a Saviour if we are to be reconciled to God. As in Romans 3: 23 – all of us have sinned and cannot be righteous without a Saviour.

God gave all people free will. God will never force a person to honour or serve Him. People must decide whether they want to know and follow God or they want to go their own way. Going their own way is anything contrary to what God gives us in His Word. God gave us the Holy Scriptures so that we would know God's will clearly about all matters for human life past, present and future. The Bible is a recording of God's dealing with man throughout various covenants – finally with Jesus Christ coming to the earth as our Saviour and bringing hope of intimacy with God in the New Covenant.

The Knowledge of Evil

We were never created to know evil or sin or the consequences of sin. Satan who started sin with his disobedience to God in heaven, was cast down to earth because of pride in his heart against God (Isaiah 14:12). Lucifer was created a beautiful covering angel that brought praise and worship to God – directly covering God's throne. Lucifer sinned by wanting to keep the glory for himself rather than give it to God. He conceived sin in himself (Angels also have free will) and wanted to keep the glory of God for himself. He wanted to be equal with God. The very sin he sinned in the presence of God, he got Adam and Eve to commit on earth.

Isaiah 14: 12 How are you fallen from heaven,
    O Lucifer, son of the morning!
How you are cut down to the ground,
    you who weaken the nations!
13 For you have said in your heart,
    "I will ascend into heaven,
I will exalt my throne
    above the stars of God;
I will sit also on the mount of the congregation,
    in the recesses of the north;
14 I will ascend above the heights of the clouds,
    I will be like the Most High."
15 Yet you shall be brought down to Hell,
    to the sides of the pit.

Satan was cast down to earth with 1/3 of the angels who followed him in rebellion against God. This was a tremendous loss of his position as he was very prominent and important in heaven. This caused him to hate God and all of God`s creation. He was not trying to help the woman and the man. He deliberately tried to ruin their intimate relationship with God. He wanted to go against God. People are deceived when they believe that any sin is more pleasurable than what God could provide. True pleasure and happiness is found in our relationship with God and in living in communion with God.

While we live on earth, there are angels both demons and angels of God who are functioning all around us. Not many people see them. Most Christians who are filled with the Holy Spirit can sense them and will respond by praying appropriately. There will be a further teaching on angels later but this is included to let you know there are humans, animals, demons and angels on earth and in the atmosphere of the earth.

Evil

People on earth are born in sin. They need a Saviour. They can do terrible things because of their sinfulness and through the demons who influence them. Examples of the consequences of evil are wars, the Holocaust, famine, sickness, death, earthquakes, human slavery, disobedience and murdering. It is hard for me to understand people who don't believe there is evil. I don`t know how they can believe that such things are natural consequences of being a human on earth.

People who choose to lie, steal, cheat, kill , murder, etc. are willfully choosing to do evil. I am naming it. Those who plot to kill people, for no reason example a terrorist attack on children in school or on people in a place of worship, or on people enjoying themselves in a café – these are things that are evil. God would never approve of it let alone inspire people to do it. Some of those very people are so truly deceived by the demons that they believe they are earning a place in heaven because of their murderous deeds. They believe that murder is God`s will. This is more than just a religious error. To believe God wants you to kill others is a direct disobedience to the commandment of God not to kill.

I live in Canada and in Canada and the United States we have laws that were formed from the Commandments of God. Yes, there are other laws that God would not approve of, but the origin of our laws is the commandments of God. Breaking the laws of man and the laws of God can never be good. I thank God that we have the freedoms that we do and I thank God that is against the law to kill or murder. Other types of evil are forcing people to do something against their will. God gave us human will; forcing someone to do something against his or her own will is a sin. Any type of harm towards a person is a sin. It is going against God's will and it is leading to consequences of death.

Romans 6: 23 For the wages of sin is death, but the gift of God is eternal life through Jesus Christ our Lord.

Sin always leads to death. The result of sin may seem temporarily pleasing, but the consequences are always death and destruction. There is some type of pleasure in sin or people wouldn't do it. The lie is that the pleasure is worth it. Nothing is worth losing your relationship with God. The lie that carnal pleasure or that any pleasure in the flesh can be beyond the pleasures of the spirit is the biggest lie. Some people believe that sin is more enjoyable than being in God's presence. They don't really know God or His presence or they would never believe that lie.

Hebrews 11: 25 choosing rather to suffer affliction with the people of God than to enjoy the pleasures of sin for a time. 26 He esteemed the reproach of Christ as greater riches than the treasures in Egypt, for he looked to the reward.

Moses chose to be identified with Hebrew slaves rather than stay in the palace of Egypt. He could have stayed and lived as a king, but inside him there was a longing to know God. Adam and Eve did not know the pleasure of what they had with God until they lost it. They could no longer walk and talk with God. They could no longer live in a heaven like garden that would have been an ultimate pleasure. The worst part of the curse is that they were no longer at one with God. They no longer knew his voice. They feared Him rather than enjoy His presence. Throughout the scriptures, the word fear is used to describe men's feelings towards God. We were the crowning achievement of God's creation

Psalm 8: For You have made him a little lower than the angels,
    and crowned him with glory and honor.

The Good News is Coming

God made us to be companions and to speak to Him openly in a glorious type of relationship. He gave us attributes like Himself such as creativity and talents and gifts that show aspects of God's awesomeness. The good news is all that was lost with the sin of Adam and Eve was restored by Christ. We who live in the present world can rejoice because

Jesus has washed and cleansed us from all sin. Jesus can take away the desire to sin by revealing His glory to us and in us. Jesus has given us total cleansing by his death burial and resurrection. Jesus paid the price for our lives so that we could be saved, healed and delivered.

The truths of Jesus are importantly called the good news because for thousands of years people on earth waited for his birth. Most of the Old Testament is dedicated to prophesying the coming of Jesus the Messiah. All of the New testament is devoted to telling us how He came and lived on earth and did signs and wonders and miracles. The ultimate gift was the giving of His life for us so that God would take His Holy sacrifice and apply it to us if we would believe on Jesus.

Please respect the human will. God gave it to you to make a choice for Him. It is the most that we as humans can give to God – our lives. Only in giving our lives to God daily, living for His glory can we know joy, peace, righteousness – the kingdom of God on the earth. Part of the good news is we don't have to wait until we get to heaven to live in the kingdom of God.

Luke 17: 20 When He was asked by the Pharisees when the kingdom of God would come, He answered them, "The kingdom of God does not come with observation. 21 Nor will they say, 'Here it is!' or 'There it is!' For remember, the kingdom of God is within you."

Entrance into The Kingdom of God

Christians are not waiting until we die to enter the kingdom of God. No. As soon as you become a Christian, you are translated – you were in the kingdom of darkness (original sin and sin) but as soon as you received Jesus Christ as Saviour, you were brought into the kingdom of light – the Kingdom of God. Christians live in the earth, but we live higher than the realms of the earth. We can be joyful, know peace, love people unconditionally and worship God because we are a part of the Kingdom of God. We live in the spirit and not in the flesh. Jesus Christ comes to live on the inside of us in the person of the Holy Spirit. God lives in us and with us.

The glory and freedom that God gives go beyond all comparison. Knowing God, the Creator of all things, loves you and cares about you, brings more joy than anything else ever could. God's plan for us is to live in joy and ecstasy in His presence. Poor substations of drugs, alcohol, sexual sin, wealth or fame attract people who have never known the pleasure of God. God's pleasure includes overwhelming peace, joy, love beyond all earthly love, fascination, comfort, communion.

Chapter self-assessment questions

1. Describe your relationship with God.
2. Describe your commitment to living for God.
3. Describe other ways you have gone rather than God's way and the consequences.

2 NOAHIC COVENANT

The covenant that God made with Noah is important because it is the first introduction of hope after Adam and Eve were made to leave Eden. It comes after a description of life on earth that sounds much like the modern world. You may have seen the movie "Noah" that was released within the last year. If you went to Sunday school, you would have been told the story of Noah and his family. It involves a global flood that covered all the earth; it was so deep that it covered the highest mountains.

Adam and Eve went on to have many children but they did not know God or serve Him. The people of the earth were doing most abominable things such as mating with demons (The Nephilim). God saw the people on earth in their wickedness and brought judgement on all the inhabitants of the earth because of it. Adam and Eve were created to be God's crowning glory but after the sin, people did not worship God. It was not until after Seth was born that people worshipped God at all. Many people were murders and killers. Sin nature and sinful choices made man fight against man.

Genesis 6: 4 The Nephilim were on the earth in those days, and also after that, when the sons of God came in to the daughters of men, and they bore children to them. These were the mighty men who were of old, men of renown.

5 The Lord saw that the wickedness of man was great on the earth, and that every intent of the thoughts of his heart was continually only evil. 6 The Lord was sorry that He had made man on the earth, and it grieved Him in His heart. 7 So the Lord said, "I will destroy man, whom I have created, from the face of the earth—both man and beast, and the creeping things, and the birds of the sky, for I am sorry that I have made them." 8 But Noah found grace in the eyes of the Lord.

Noah Found Favour with God

God saw that Noah was a person He could speak with. Noah was a just man and blameless among his contemporaries. He had three sons: Ham, Shem and Japheth. Noah wasn't perfect but compared to the people around him, he was the person God spoke to about a new covenant. God's covenants are God's attempts to make agreements or peace with man. God loved mankind – and provided a hope in His covenant. Noah was a person who walked with God; Noah sought God and wanted to serve Him.

God is Holy and He hates sin. He saw the wickedness of men and wanted to destroy all of the earth because of it, but He had mercy on Noah and his family by offering them a hope. The Covenant God was making with Noah follows:

Genesis 6: 13 So God said to Noah, "The end of all flesh is come before Me, for the earth is filled with violence because of them. Now I will destroy them with the earth. 14 Make an ark of cypress wood for yourself. Make rooms in the ark, and cover it inside and out with pitch. 15 And this is how you must make it: The length of the ark will be three hundred cubits, the width of it fifty cubits, and the height of it thirty cubits.[a] 16 Make an opening[b] one cubit[c] below the top of the ark all around; and you must set the door of the ark on the side. Make it with a lower, a second, and a third story. 17 I will bring a flood of waters on the earth to destroy all flesh, wherever there is the breath of life under heaven, and everything that is on the earth will die. 18 But I will establish My covenant with you; you must go into the ark—you, and your sons, and your wife, and your sons' wives with you. 19 Bring every living thing of all flesh, two of every kind, into the ark to keep them alive with you. They shall be male and female. 20 Two of every kind of bird, of every kind of animal, and of every kind of creeping thing of the earth will come to you to be kept alive. 21 Also, take with you of every kind of food that is eaten and gather it to yourself, and it will be for food for you and for them."

The Ark of Safety

Noah was to build an ark for safety for he and his family and the animals that God instructed him to bring. God gave Noah the blueprints or the knowledge of how to create it so that it would be a shelter for them. Until this point, it had never rained on earth. Water as a mist would come up from the ground and water the plants. God promised to do a new thing. Please realize that Noah had to believe God because he had never seen rain and had never built a boat before. It was completely obeying God's instructions by faith, without any prior knowledge of anything God was speaking about. I'm quite sure Noah saw the wicked people around him because it Noah sought God. Noah wanted to serve God. God instructed Noah to build a huge boat. It was to be big enough to hold all of the animals: mostly 2 of a kind except some animals extra for food and sacrifice.

Building the Ark

There is a place in Kentucky in the United States, where you can view and go on a life size built to scale model of the ark. It is huge. It took Noah 120 years to build the ark and during his building of it he was preaching to any of the people who passed him and wanted to know what he was doing. The people mocked Noah because of his faith and his building of something they could not understand. It would be hard to believe in rain if you have never seen it or experienced it. It would be hard to believe that life might not exist the way they knew it. It would be tough enough for a righteous person to believe. Most certainly those who mocked God and lived in sin would not obey or help to build the ark. In all those years, only Noah's immediate family believed.

1 Peter 3: 20 who in times past were disobedient, when God waited patiently in the days of Noah while the ark was being prepared, in which a few, that is, eight souls, were saved through water.

Noah and his sons built the ark. It was no easy task because tools were primitive and they had to cut down the trees, make lumber and construct the boat. God promised it would rain for forty days and forty nights (Genesis 7). God warned Noah that all people and animals outside the ark were going to die.

Genesis 7: 4 In seven days I will cause it to rain on the earth for forty days and forty nights, and every living thing that I have made I will destroy from the face of the earth." After Noah had built the ark and is was completed, the animals came to the ark. I'm not sure if an angel of the LORD lead them or God simply called them, but the animals came.

Genesis 7: 6 Noah was six hundred years old when the floodwaters came upon the earth. 7 And Noah went with his sons and his wife and his sons' wives into the ark because of the floodwaters. 8 Everything that creeps on the land from clean and unclean animals and birds 9 came in two by two, male and female, to Noah into the ark, as God had commanded Noah. 10 After seven days, the waters of the flood were on the earth.

Entrance into the Ark

Genesis 7: 5 And Noah did according to all that the Lord commanded him.

Noah and his family also entered the ark. The scripture refers to the fountains of the deep and the flood gates of heaven being opened. Water was coming from within the earth; water was coming from the heavens. There was water in such an abundance as had never been on the earth before.

There was only one window in the ark and God sealed the door. Noah could not have opened that door if he wanted to because God sealed it. There are seasons where a door of opportunity may come to people and they are given a chance of escape. It can be as with Noah and the flood or it can be in the present. There are some people who don't accept Christ now because they say "maybe near the end of my life" so they can enjoy their lives in sin, repent at the last minute of their lives and still get to heaven. The truth is none of us knows when the door will be shut by God.

The Door

This is one of the reasons I keep praying for some people to be saved, that God would have mercy and give them a new chance to receive Jesus Christ as Saviour. One day though will come when the last chance will be given to the person. It will be a destiny decision. The person can repent and come to Jesus Christ, or the person can say no and not know Christ and die. What I am saying is only God can give doors of such opportunity. Please remember to pray for those in your life that do not know Christ that God would have mercy on them and give them a new opportunity, that God would soften their hearts so that they might be saved. Even though God loves all people, He will never force people to accept Him. Noah didn't capture people, tie them and throw them in the ark. Noah didn't force people into the ark. God wants people to come to come because they choose Him. They must choose God of their own free will.

Faith

Hebrews 11: 7 By faith Noah, being divinely warned about things not yet seen, moved with godly fear, prepared an ark to save his family, by which he condemned the world and became an heir of the righteousness that comes by faith.

Noah and his family were inside of the ark without being able to see what was going on outside. This emphasized Noah's faith in God. I'm sure they could hear people banging on the door wanting to get in. I'm sure they could hear cries of peoples and animals as the water got higher.

It was most certainly a judgement upon all of mankind. Many people may believe it is without reason but God knew that of all the families on earth, only one had faith in God. Noah's family and the animals chosen were to repopulate the earth. God cared that He saved some of each of the animal species. God cared that he kept Noah and his family. He didn't destroy all the earth and all people and animals. A remnant was kept. The remnant represented hope for life and covenant with God.

Life in the Ark

To be in an enclosed space that had no natural light, hearing the water rushing all around you, being tossed with the waves, and being with all of those animals who required food and water, and only your family would have been an experience of faith. They knew what was going on. They had to believe that God would keep His promise and cause the rain to cease. It might not have been tough the first day or the first week, but after a month, I'm sure they all wanted to get out of that confined space and be able to see the sky. All that they knew was completely washed away.

The face of the earth was transformed so that water was where it had never been before. There would have been mudslides and earthquakes as the fountains of the earth gushed as well as the waters of the heavens. They were in a place of safety but it was not a place of ease because they had never experienced this voyage and did not know what to expect. It meant total faith in God who promised to keep His covenant.

For 150 days, the waters prevailed. That is more than four months of being in an enclosed area with all those animals and only what they could see in front of them and the promise that God would keep His promise to end the rain. After those 150 days, the flood began to recede or end. The fountains of the deep were closed and the floodgates were also closed by God. The rain had finally ended.

Genesis 8: 4 The ark rested in the seventh month, on the seventeenth day of the month, on the mountains of Ararat.

There is evidence of an ark on Mt. Ararat. There are pictures and some scientists were able to secure some photos in 2006 and 2007, but they were stopped by the people of modern day Iraq. The country will not permit any scientific exploration of the region.

After the rains stopped, there was still much water that had to be soaked up and separated into oceans etc. Noah opened the window of the ark and released a bird – a Raven to go to find land. The Bible doesn't say the raven came back. Afterwards, he released a dove. The dove returned because she could not find a tree or resting place. Noah waited seven more days and released the dove again.

Genesis 8: 11 The dove came to him in the evening, and in her mouth, there was a freshly plucked olive leaf. So Noah knew that the waters had receded from the earth. 12 He waited another seven days and sent out the dove again, but it did not return to him again.

The dove's return with the olive branch meant there was new life, new growth, hope for the earth. The dove was going to start building a nest.

Genesis 8: 13 So in the six hundred and first year, in the first month, the first day of the month, the waters were dried up from the earth; and Noah removed the covering of the ark, and looked, and saw the surface of the ground was dry. 14 In the second month, on the twenty-seventh day of the month, the earth was dry.

The waters had finally dried up. Freedom came as God instructed Noah to leave the ark. God had kept His promise. They had lived through a most horrible storm but all of them were safe.

Genesis 8: 13 So in the six hundred and first year, in the first month, the first day of the month, the waters were dried up from the earth; and Noah removed the covering of the ark, and looked, and saw the surface of the ground was dry. 14 In the second month, on the twenty-seventh day of the month, the earth was dry.

God gave them permission to exit the ark. God commanded them to replenish the earth. That means God wanted them to reproduce, to fill the earth with people and animals.

Genesis 8: 15 Then God spoke to Noah, saying, 16 "Go out of the ark, you and your wife, and your sons and your sons' wives with you. 17 Bring out with you every living thing of all flesh that is with you, birds and animals, and every creeping thing that creeps on the earth, so that they may breed abundantly on the earth and be fruitful and multiply on the earth."

One of the first things that Noah did was build an altar to worship God. He offered animal sacrifice and God was pleased. God made a promise to Noah and to all living creatures that never again would he destroy all the people or all the animals. Never again would He destroy the earth – but in fact there would be seasons as long as the earth remained.

Genesis 8: 20 Then Noah built an altar to the Lord and took of every clean animal and of every clean bird and offered burnt offerings on the altar. 21 The Lord smelled a soothing aroma; and the Lord said in His heart, "I will never again curse the ground because of man, for the inclination of man's heart is evil from his youth, nor will I again destroy every living thing as I have done.

22 While the earth remains,
seedtime and harvest,
cold and heat,
summer and winter,
and day and night
will not cease."

The final part of the Noahtic covenant is the final part of the promise. God would never again destroy all of creatures, He promised people. He promised animals.

Genesis 9: 8 Again God spoke to Noah and to his sons with him, saying, 9 "As for Me, I establish My covenant with you, and with your descendants after you; 10 and with every living creature that is with you, the birds, the livestock, and every beast of the earth with you; of all that comes out of the ark, every beast of the earth. 11 I establish My covenant with you. Never again shall all flesh be cut off by the waters of a flood. Never again shall there be a flood to destroy the earth."

12 Then God said, "This is the sign of the covenant which I am making between Me and you and every living creature that is with you, for all future generations. 13 I have set My rainbow in the cloud, and it shall be a sign of a covenant between Me and the earth. 14 When I bring a cloud over the earth, the rainbow will be seen in the cloud; 15 then I will remember My covenant, which is between Me and you and every living creature of all flesh, and the waters will never again become a flood to destroy all flesh. 16 The rainbow will appear in the cloud, and I will see it and remember the everlasting covenant between God and every living creature of all flesh that is on the earth."

Conditions of the Noahtic Covenant

The conditions of this new covenant were fulfilled as God placed a rainbow in the sky. It is an eternal sign of God's promise to us that never again would the earth be flooded or such judgement against all creation be done. God gave them special instruction that they could eat of the animals but must not drink or eat the blood. This is essential because later He gives the same commandment to Moses. Also, for the shedding of blood, a person must die. God stated that a murderer must did for his sin. This is also later given to Moses. God made this covenant with Noah, with all of his descendants and with all the future generations including you and I. The rainbow should confirm to us God's faithfulness to His promises to Noah and to us.

Chapter summary Questions

1. The symbol or a rainbow is given. Explain the significance.
2. Describe the symbol of the ark of safety with the New Testament or Covenant with Jesus Christ.
3. Describe the qualities you believe Noah and his family had.

3 ABRAHAMIC COVENANT

Abrahamic Covenant : God reveals Himself

Abraham is an important part of our heritage. There are movies about his life. He is a hero of faith because of his life committed to God. Abraham was a man chosen by God. Abraham was a good man chosen to be the founder of Israel. He did not know God, until God spoke to him. He lived in Ur of the Chaldees a place known for idolatry. There has been modern excavation of that region and there are some structures and artifacts that remain from this civilization. God revealed himself to Abraham and gave him instruction that seemed ridiculous. Abraham was doing well financially in his life. He had married Sarai but was childless. He was in hos 70's when he chose to obey God's instruction to him.

Genesis 12 : 1 Now the LORD said to Abram, "Go from your country, your family, and your father's house to the land that I will show you, 2 I will make of you a great nation;
I will bless you
and make your name great,
so that you will be a blessing.
3 I will bless them who bless you
and curse him who curses you,[a]
and in you all families of the earth
will be blessed."

Please understand that God called Abraham to leave all his family and his position and all he knew to go to a place uncertain. The only sure thing was that God promised to lead him. It is hard for us to compare this request to any modern request. He was called out of all that he knew that was prospering him so that God could make him a great nation. This in itself must have seemed intangible to Abraham. If he thought of it with his intellect, it would have seemed ridiculous. He must have wondered how could God make a nation from him if his wife could not have children. God promised to bless those that were good to Him and to curse them that were his enemies. This is the start of the Abrahamic covenant. He obeyed God. Even though he was prospering where he was, he packed up his wife and all his herds and goods and obeyed God.

Most surely his family members would have wanted to know where he was going. Abraham had to answer by saying, God will show me the place. Surely, they wanted to know which god had spoken to him. He could only reply it was the one true God. I'm sure his family did not understand because they did not know God. Part of the reason God called him out from among them is so that God could teach Abraham about faith and about living by God's provision. I'm not sure any of us would leave all that we know without knowing the place of destiny. Our nation of Canada has many refugees who come to this nation because of the freedoms we have here. They know their destiny is Canada. Abraham did not know his destiny; he only knew he had heard the one true God directing him with a promise of making a nation from him.

Hebrews 11: 8 By faith Abraham obeyed when he was called to go out into a place which he would later receive as an inheritance. He went out not knowing where he was going. 9 By faith he dwelt in the promised land, as in a foreign land, dwelling in tents with Isaac and Jacob, the heirs of the same promise, 10 for he was looking for a city which has foundations, whose builder and maker is God.

Even though Noah was a good man, many people did not know the LORD God as Noah did. People were given to worshipping idols of stone or wood or other things. Mankind was not following the God of Noah. The demons did not die in the flood as evil men and women did. They found other people and seduced them to worship false gods. After the life of Noah, people were given to following idols.

God Changed their Names

God saw Abraham as a man he could make covenant with. Abraham's name was Abram – God later changed his name. Sarah's name was Sarai; God later changed her name. God changed their names because of the covenant He made with Abraham. It meant not only identification on earth but identification with God and an abundance of promise in the spiritual realm also. God spoke to Abram and told him the changes of their name.

Genesis 17: 5 No longer will your name be called Abram, but your name will be Abraham, for I have made you the father of a multitude of nations. 6 I will make you exceedingly fruitful; and I will make nations of you, and kings will come from you. 7 I will establish My covenant between Me and you and your descendants after you throughout their generations for an everlasting covenant, to be God to you and your descendants after you.

Sarah must have been a beautiful woman – beyond normal beauty.

Once Abraham and Sarai, at the ages of about 70, got to Gerar, Abraham lied saying Sarai was his sister and not his wife, because he feared that the king might desire her and kill Ahraham because of his desire for Sarai.

Genesis 20: 1 Abraham journeyed from there toward the Negev, settled between Kadesh and Shur, and then he sojourned in Gerar. 2 Then Abraham said about Sarah his wife, "She is my sister." So Abimelek, king of Gerar, sent for her and took Sarah.

3 But God came to Abimelek in a dream by night and said to him, "You are a dead man because of the woman whom you have taken, for she is a man's wife."

4 Abimelek had not gone near her, and he said, "Lord, will You slay a righteous nation? 5 Did he not say to me, 'She is my sister,' and did not even she herself say, 'He is my brother'? In the integrity of my heart and innocence of my hands I have done this."

6 And God said to him in a dream, "Yes, I know that you did this in the integrity of your heart. For I also kept you from sinning against Me. Therefore, I did not let you touch her. 7 Therefore return the man's wife, for he is a prophet and he will pray for you. Moreover, you will live. However, if you do not return her, know that you will surely die, you and all who are yours."

It happens that king Abimelech does desire Sarai and separates her to join his haram. God honoured Abraham even though Abraham is a coward (rather to lose his wife than his life) and a deceiver (lied to protect his own life). God warns the king that Sarai is Abraham's wife. The king of course fears God and says he is innocent. God not only reveals himself to a king that did not know God but protects Abraham because of the covenant he has with him. His wife Sarai is part of the plan of blessing Abraham and God protects her.

God's promise of blessing was on Abraham and his children and their children would be blessed. This is an awesome blessing should God speak it to you and you have many children. God was speaking it to a man and woman who had no children and who were quite old; this is the realm of divine promise for the miraculous to occur.

Genesis 15: 5 He brought him outside and said, "Look up toward heaven and count the stars, if you are able to count them." And He said to him, "So will your descendants be."

6 Abram believed the Lord, and He credited it to him as righteousness.

Abraham 22: 17 I will indeed bless you and I will indeed multiply your descendants as the stars of the heavens and as the sand that is on the seashore. Your descendants will possess the gate of their enemies. 18 Through your offspring all the nations of the earth will be blessed, because you have obeyed My voice."

God's promises

God promises him so many heirs and offspring, that worship and serve God, that they are too numerous to count – an overwhelming number. The promise that God would multiply his descendants was the core of the Abrahamic covenant. It was a promise that caused Abraham and Sarah to believe the for a miracle. The blessing of him meant physically, financially, spiritually. God's promise of blessing him was evident in how he was treated and how God provided for them and prospered them, even though they did not have family wherever they went. Lot, his nephew, wanted to go with him and he followed his uncle in the early part of Abraham's journey to the land that God promised him. The promised land that God would give to the descendants of Abraham is Israel. Jacob who is a descendent of Abraham was renamed by God as Israel; he is the founder of the nation of Israel. Through Abraham comes Israel and Ishmael and all of the nations he founded, most Arabic nations.

The blessings of Abraham by God included that wherever Abraham would go, God would prosper him and all those around him (Genesis 28: 15). These promises are still true for the children of Abraham – all Jewish peoples and Christians who inherit the promises of Abraham by faith. Jesus Christ, a descendent of Israel makes it possible for Christians to receive the fullness of the blessings given to Abraham. Jesus Christ not only started a new covenant but sealed and secured all of the other covenants so that we who believe in Jesus become heirs of the promises of God to all his people.

Galatians 3: 14 so that the blessing of Abraham might come on the Gentiles through Jesus Christ, that we might receive the promise of the Spirit through faith.

The Promises to Abraham

God chose to place special blessing on Abraham's descendant with Isaac being the seed of promise. Ismael is also blessed because he is of

Abraham's seed but he is not the chosen seed. Isaac was chosen as the one to carry on the Abrahamic covenant. Literally, if you curse or fight against Jewish people, God has promised to curse you and fight against you (Genesis 12: 3). God has a special promise upon Israel because of the covenant with Abraham.

Christians, are made an heir of Abraham by faith in Jesus Christ. God promises him that kings will come forth from him and that he will always be victorious over any enemy. Abraham's part of the covenant was that he had to believe God. He had to believe for the impossible. He had to believe that God would provide for him. He had to believe that God would keep His word. No evidence of the children occurred for almost twenty years after Abraham followed God. That is a long duration to wait to inherit a promise. That took some faith. He had to know that he heard from God to believe that God would keep this promise although it didn't fully manifest in his life.

The first part of the fulfillment blessing was the birth of his children who would be founders of mighty nations. Abraham though carried the promises by faith throughout his life although he only saw the promise of a multitude of people that would be his inhabitants by faith in God and His promises.

Abraham had special relationship with God because of these covenant blessings discussed, but please know Abraham didn't have the abiding presence of God living on the inside of him to encourage him and build him up spiritually. You and I can talk to God directly 24/7. Abraham sought God and made altars of sacrifice to him but He did not have the intimate communion that we can have with God through the indwelling Holy Spirit. God did come and talk to Abraham but it was on certain occasions. Abraham had to keep those words God spoke to him by faith. He had to put total faith in what God spoke to him.

O, what we take for granted. You and I can talk to God 24/7. God is always with us. His presence is with us. The Holy Spirit speaks with us and prompts us and encourages us. The Holy Spirit teaches us and reminds us of what God has spoken to us. There is nothing stopping us from approaching God's throne to speak to Him because Jesus blood gives us entrance into the Holy of Holies in heaven. God made a way for us to directly hear from God and to live in communion with Him.

Abraham's faith was attributed to him as righteousness. Abraham's faith was to see the plan of God in spirit by faith before he saw any evidence of it on the earth. He believed what God has promised him, God would do even though it was by all natural means impossible.

Romans 4: 18 Against all hope, he believed in hope, that he might become the father of many nations according to what was spoken, "So shall your descendants be."[d] 19 And not being weak in faith, he did not consider his own body to be dead (when he was about a hundred years old), nor yet the deadness of Sarah's womb. 20 He did not waver at the promise of God through unbelief, but was strong in faith, giving glory to God, 21 and being fully persuaded that what God had promised, He was able to perform. 22 Therefore "it was credited to him as righteousness."

The Special Manifestation of God's Covenant to Abraham

God manifests Himself to Abraham in a unique way. Abraham had been offering animal sacrifices, building an altar to worship God but there is a unique manifestation of God coming to Abraham in a covenant of sacrifice. God gives him instruction of what to do to bring a sacrifice – an altar or entrance point of speaking with God. He had to follow God's instructions very clearly. He cut the animal parts in halves as God commanded him. He chased away any animal that tried to come near. This was a physical sign of the covenant. God caused Abraham to go into a deep sleep. God spoke to Him in this way and promised him once more about his descendants.

Genesis 15: 7 He also said to him, "I am the Lord who brought you out of Ur of the Chaldeans to give you this land to possess[b] it."

8 But Abram said, "Lord God, how may I know that I will possess it?"

9 So He said to him, "Bring Me a three-year-old heifer, a three-year-old female goat, a three-year-old ram, a turtledove, and a young pigeon."

10 Then Abram brought all of these to Him and cut them in two and laid each piece opposite the other, but he did not cut the birds in half. 11 When the birds of prey came down on the carcasses, Abram drove them away.

12 As the sun was going down, a deep sleep fell on Abram, and terror and a great darkness fell on him. 13 Then He said to Abram, "Know for certain that your descendants will live as strangers in a land that is not theirs, and they will be enslaved and mistreated for four hundred years. 14 But I will judge the nation that they serve, and afterward they will come out with great possessions. 15 As for you, you will go to your fathers in peace and you will

be buried at a good old age. 16 In the fourth generation, your descendants will return here, for the iniquity of the Amorites is not yet complete."

17 When the sun went down and it was dark, a smoking fire pot with a flaming torch passed between these pieces. 18 On that same day the Lord made a covenant with Abram, saying, "To your descendants I have given this land, from the river of Egypt to the great Euphrates River— 19 the land of the Kenites, the Kenizzites, the Kadmonites, 20 the Hittites, the Perizzites, the Rephaites, 21 the Amorites, the Canaanites, the Girgashites, and the Jebusites."

God physically came down in presence to make covenant with Abraham. God's presence (the flaming torch) passed between the animals cut in half and it was a sign of true covenant with Abraham as God's presence was there with him in a ceremony that God ordained. God gives him a prophetic word about his descendants who would be born and gives him knowledge of their destiny in the distant future including the captivity in Egypt for 400 years and their deliverance from it. He promises Abraham will live a long fruitful life and see peace all his days. He names all the people groups that were inhabiting the lands of Canaan and promises all that land to Abraham and his descendants. This unique manifestation of the Abrahamic covenant is a physical demonstration of God's faithfulness to keep His promises to Abraham.

This experience seals God's promises to Abraham. Abraham knows he has experienced something supernatural. God's confirmation of all He has said in the past and foretelling of the future of Abraham's descendants is a manifestation of God's mercy towards him.

When people used to make a covenant they would not only cut their arm until they mingled their blood but they would cut in half in the animals as a sacrifice and walk between them as a promise that if either of them were to not keep his promise, their bodies should be as those animals – it was a walk through the animal sacrifices that sealed their promise – it was a promise or vow unto death. This is what God does with Abraham saying He will keep His covenant with the physical carcasses of animals, so that it was engrained into Abraham's memory. This was a faith injection. It was a most solemn oath that God made with Abraham that day.

Childless

Remember, Abraham is in his 70's and he does not even have one child yet. He has the promise of God but does not have an heir. Sarah cannot have children and here she is 70 years old, past the years of bearing children. It seems impossible for God to keep His promise to Abraham. God promises that Abraham and Sarah would be the parents of all the children of Israel, yet they have no child.

Sign of the Covenant of Abraham

The sign of the covenant for Abraham and their descendants was that they would have to circumcise all their males. It is literally the cutting of the foreskin of the penis. It is a physical alteration in the males` body as a sign they believed God and honoured God and His promises to Abraham. It is usually done as the children are babies because it is less painful. Many Jewish people still do this as a sign of the covenant today. Many Christians also do it. It has benefits that are healthy, for cleanliness etc. The main purpose is that it is an outward sign in the physical body showing faith towards the covenant God made with Abraham. If they refused circumcision, they were to be killed. They could have no part in Abraham`s covenant or blessings if they did not obey this physical requirement.

Genesis 17: 9 Then God said to Abraham, "As for you, you shall keep My covenant, you and your descendants after you throughout their generations. 10 This is My covenant, which you shall keep, between Me and you and your descendants after you; every male among you shall be circumcised. 11 You shall circumcise the flesh of your foreskins, and it shall be a sign of the covenant between Me and you. 12 Every male throughout every generation that is eight days old shall be circumcised, whether born in your household or bought with money from a foreigner who is not your descendant. 13 He who is born in your house and he who is bought with your money must be circumcised. My covenant shall be in your flesh as an everlasting covenant. 14 Any uncircumcised male whose flesh of his foreskin is not circumcised shall be cut off from his people. He has broken My covenant."

Abraham obeyed God and both he and his son Ishmael were circumcised and all the males that were with Abraham.

Sarah`s Inspiration to help God

Sarah had a servant girl, named Hagar and she was faithful. Sarah knew of the promises of God to her husband but she knew she was barren and she knew she was past the years of bearing children. She decided to help fulfill the promise of God to Abraham by giving Hagar, her servant, to be a surrogate mother to a child of Abraham. Please know this was a moment of sincerely believing it was a good idea to help God. No other woman would get her husband to have sex with her maid. It also showed that Sarah did not have the same relationship with God that Abraham did. She did not simply believe; she believed but thought that she must take part in it for it to occur.

Genesis 16: 16 Now Sarai, Abram's wife, had borne him no children, and she had a maidservant, an Egyptian, whose name was Hagar. 2 So Sarai said to Abram, "The Lord has prevented me from having children. Please go in to my maid; it may be that I will obtain children through her."

Abram listened to Sarai. 3 So after Abram had been living for ten years in the land of Canaan, Sarai, his wife, took Hagar her maid, the Egyptian, and gave her to her husband Abram to be his wife. 4 He went in to Hagar, and she conceived.

The Bible describes Sarah's jealousy over Hagar and there was strife among them. Hagar is treated unkindly and runs away. An angel of the LORD appears to her and gives her a prophesy. Ishmael would also be blessed of God because the blessing of God was on Abraham and all his seed. This comforts Hagar and she returns and delivers the child. Abraham raises the child.

Genesis 16: 11 Then the angel of the Lord said to her,

"You are pregnant
    and will bear a son.
You shall call his name Ishmael,
    because the Lord has heard your affliction.
12 He will be a wild man;
    his hand will be against every man,
    and every man's hand will be against him.
And he will dwell
    in the presence of all his brothers."

Abraham circumcises Ishmael and God speaks to him so that he might clearly understand that the blessing of God was on Sarah to become the mother of nations. Please understand that now Abraham and Sarah are in their 90's. It is completely naturally impossible for Sarah to have children but God promised, and Abraham believed God. God gives him the name he is to call his son. God assures him that Isaac will be the son who inherits the promises God has made to Abraham. He also places a blessing on Ishmael – but it is not in the same measure.

Genesis 17: 15 Then God said to Abraham, "As for Sarai your wife, you will not call her name Sarai, but her name will be Sarah. 16 I will bless her and also give you a son by her. I will bless her, and she will be the mother of nations. Kings of peoples will come from her."

19 Then God said, "No, but your wife Sarah will bear you a son, and you will call his name Isaac. I will establish My covenant with him as an everlasting covenant and with his descendants after him. 20 And as for Ishmael, I have heard you. I have blessed him, and will make him fruitful and will multiply him exceedingly. He will be the father of twelve princes, and I will make him a great nation. 21 But I will establish My covenant with Isaac, whom Sarah will bear to you at this set time next year." 22 Then He stopped talking with Abraham, and God went up from

Because of Hagar and Sarah's strife, there is not a good atmosphere in the camp. Soon after, some visitors arrive. Abraham shows hospitality and generosity towards these men. Abraham does not realize these are messengers from God until they ask about his wife Sarah.

Genesis 18: 10 One of them said, "I will certainly return to you about this time next year, and Sarah your wife will have a son."

And Sarah heard it in the tent door, which was behind him. 11 Now Abraham and Sarah were old and very advanced in age, and Sarah was well past childbearing. 12 Therefore Sarah laughed to herself, saying, "After I am so old and my lord is old also, shall I have pleasure?"

13 Then the Lord said to Abraham, "Why did Sarah laugh and say, 'Shall I surely bear a child when I am old?' 14 Is anything too difficult for the Lord? At the appointed time I will return to you, at this time next year, and Sarah will have a son."

God promised through these messengers that Sarah would give birth. Sarah laughs because she knows it is not earthly possible. Within one year, Sarah gives birth to Isaac while she is in her 90's. God keeps His promise to Abraham.

Genesis 21: 2 For Sarah conceived and bore Abraham a son in his old age, at the set time that God had spoken to him. 3 Abraham called the name of his son who was born to him, whom Sarah bore to him, Isaac. 4 Then Abraham circumcised his son Isaac when he was eight days old, as God had commanded him. 5 Now Abraham was one hundred years old when his son Isaac was born to him.

It is shortly after the birth of Isaac the son of promise that Sarah drives Hagar and her son away. Abraham is hesitant but obeys God because God makes it clear that it should be that Ishmael to depart. This must have been pretty tough on him because it was his son who he raised as his son. He loved him but what seems to be very important in the life of Abraham, and in our lives, is that only certain people should be with him. Other people are not to be there. People add to your faith or they do not. There are people often included in the miraculous manifestations of God to people in the Old and New Testaments. There is a clear separating of the people of faith and the people who are good – not of the same faith.

Genesis 21: 12 But God said to Abraham, "Do not be upset concerning the boy and your slave wife. Whatever Sarah has said to you, listen to what she says, for in Isaac your descendants will be called. 13 Yet I will also make a nation of the son of the slave woman, because he is your offspring."

God Opens Wombs

God is a God who can do the impossible. He kept His promises to Abraham even though it seemed completely impossible in the natural realm. God honoured his covenant with Abraham by opening Sarah's womb to give birth to a child. The same God who did it thousands of years ago, does still do it today. I have met so many people who have shared with me that it was impossible for them to have children, yet God made a way.

In some instances all the female sexual parts were not in proper working condition, but God made a way. If someone has told you that you cannot have children, please go to God in faith believing that what He did for Sarah, He can do for you today. Go to somebody of faith, who will pray with you and for you that your womb will be opened so you can have a child. I have known of certain people who had a special anointing in this area. These people prayed with women who could not have children and their wombs were open and they had children. Remember it must be a prayer of faith. If you do not believe, it's not worth doing.

Hebrews 11: 6 And without faith it is impossible to please God, for he who comes to God must believe that He exists and that He is a rewarder of those who diligently seek Him.

Sodom and Gomorrah

Those messengers that prophesied to Abraham and Sarah also shared with Abraham they were on a mission from God to examine the region of Sodom and Gomorrah. They believed wickedness was there and they were told to destroy the place if it were true. First of all, you must know Abraham was a special servant of God because God shared with him God's plans. Abraham's nephew who had come with them, soon found out he liked money and gathering wealth than the company of his uncle Abraham. Lot went to live in the region of Sodom and Gomorrah so he could do business there. The Bible doesn't say that Lot was doing the sexual sins and idolatry of Sodom and Gomorrah, but he was surely lead by his covetousness for wealth rather than his love for God because he brought his family to such a region of wickedness.

Abraham cared for his family member even though he didn't approve of him. Abraham knew the region was wicked and begged the messengers not to destroy the place if there were righteous people there. God agreed if there were 10 righteous people in Sodom Gomorrah, He would not destroy them. The truth is, there were no righteous people in that area. The only people worth delivering out of that region were Lot and his wife and two daughters. Even their husbands wouldn't go.

The people were given to violence and sexual sins, covetousness and pride. The angels deliver Lot's family from this region but Lot's wife died when she disobeyed God. God had told them not to look back because God was destroying the place and people they had known. Lot's wife turned and was turned into a pillar of salt. Only Lot and his 2 daughters escaped (Genesis 19). Rather than return to Abraham who worshipped God, Lot begged to stay in a pagan city so he could do business with the people there (Zoar) who worshipped idols.

I believe God spared Lot because of His covenant with Abraham not because of Lot's relationship with God. God so honoured Abraham that he spared his family members from judgement.

Outward Signs of God's Covenant With Abraham

Every place that Abraham went he was blessed, wealthy, prosperous. God had given him earthly blessing with all kinds of herds and possessions. He had kept his promise and given him an heir in Isaac. Abraham has long life, health, children, is dwelling in the land God promised to give him. Abraham has a strong relationship with God. He has experienced the miraculous and all seems to be fulfilled. It is at the height of his celebrating inheriting all God's promises that this next thing occurs. God gives Abraham a special request – it is hard for anyone to conceive of it as being possibly from God. It has only occurred once with Abraham. God asked Abraham to bring his son Isaac and offer him as a sacrifice on an altar to God (Genesis 22: 2). Please know – in no other place in scripture will you see God asking for a blood sacrifice from a human.

Genesis 22: 2 Then He said, "Take your son, your only son Isaac, whom you love, and go to the land of Moriah, and offer him there as a burnt offering on one of the mountains of which I will tell you."

Please know how hard it must have been for Abraham to willingly obey God. He knew that God had prophesied that Isaac would be the one who all the nation of Israel would come through. He knew Isaac was a special miracle to them. He obeyed God. Abraham brings his son to the mountain and lays him on the altar. He is ready to take a knife to slay him. This shows in all ways Abraham would have gone through with it. At that moment of the knife being raised, God spoke to Abraham and stopped him.

Genesis 22: 12 Then He said, "Do not lay your hands on the boy or do anything to him, because now I know that you fear God, seeing you have not withheld your only son from Me."

The Sacrifice

A ram caught in the bush was given as the sacrifice instead. Both God and Abraham and Isaac knew that Abraham loved God and was sworn to keep his covenant with God more than loving or holding on to anything on earth. I do not believe this is only to test Abrahams faith. It is also a foreshadow of what Jehovah God does for us thousands of years later in the person of Jesus Christ who died so that we might be saved. I believe it was a fulfilling of what God was willing to do. As certain as Abraham would have given his son to God, God gave His son to fulfill all promises to Abraham. We, through Jesus Christ, that we who were Gentiles without hope in knowing God could inherit the blessings of Abraham through faith in Jesus Christ.

John 3: 16 "For God so loved the world that He gave His only begotten Son, that whoever believes in Him should not perish, but have eternal life.

The special call of God on Abraham was to leave all that He knew believing by faith that God would give him what God promised. He obeyed God in all ways and inherited the promises. It involved faith and an outward sign in their physical body (circumcision) to show they honour

God. All Jewish peoples are the descendants of Abraham through Isaac. All Arabic peoples are the inheritance of Abraham through Ishmael. We who are not from this heritage, being gentiles of people outside of the covenant are made partakers of the covenant through faith in Jesus Christ. Jesus blood shed for us, makes us joint heirs of the promises of Abraham.

Because of Christ, we can be a people fruitful and prosperous. We can have children who will honour God and serve Him. We can leave descendants with a legacy of faith honouring God.

End of Chapter Questions

1. Describe your encounter of hearing God.
2. Explain how taking with God has changed your life.
3. What person in your family was the first Christian?
4. Describe how the first Christian's life impacted your family.

4 MOSAIC COVENANT

Mosaic Covenant

Most people know the Mosaic Covenant as the commandments that were given to Moses by God. It includes those commandments but also includes more; there are 613 commandments that God gave to Moses for Israel. Moses was also given plans by God to build a place of worship – a tabernacle including the ark of the covenant where God's presence would dwell.

Moses

There have been several movies about the deliverance of Israel out of Egypt, of Moses the prophet of God who God used to do mighty miracles. Remember Abraham had been given the details of how Israel would be in captivity for 400 years. Moses was born in a Jewish home during the captivity. The Pharaoh made a proclamation that all Jewish baby boys were to be killed. This would have included Moses.

Moses mother hid him as long as she could but knew that his life was in danger. What she did is place him in a basket of reeds that was pitched with tar to make it waterproof. She had Miriam, Moses' sister, place the basket in the river Nile and they prayed over his life. What happened is the basket was carried near to the Princess of Egypt's bathing area and she found the child and raised him as her own son. Miriam spoke with the princess and Moses own mother was hired to care for the child. He got the best education, the best food, best training and was raised as a prince in Egypt. He lived this way until he was forty years old.

Egypt was a powerful nation; they had an advanced civilization. For forty years, Moses lived in luxury living in a palace knowing life from a prince of Egypt's perspective. At forty years, he saw one Israelite being abused, physically beaten, by an Egyptian. This would have been normal in Egypt because the Israelites were slaves. The Egyptians were terrible task masters. The Bible says that their cry for help rose up to God. Seeing the Egyptian beating the slave bothered Moses so much that he interrupted and tried to stop it – and did stop it but he had killed the Egyptian during the confrontation. Moses hid the body of the Egyptian in the sand. This was not a wise thing because of the winds that blew in the region; the body was discovered and Moses was pronounced guilty of murder. Moses was banished from Egypt. That means he lost all of his position and authority and was released to the Sinai desert.

After 40 years of luxury, suddenly he was in the wilderness alone. He made his way through the desert and found Jethro a Midianite shepherd and his daughters. He was welcomed by them to become as one of them. The next 40 years of Moses life, he spends as a shepherd. He marries and has children (Exodus 2: 11-25). He learns what it is to work as a shepherd and a completely different life style of living in tents and moving to green pastures to care for the sheep and goats. He learns that the Midianites were Ishmael's people and believed in the same God of Abraham. We don't know too much but we know that Jethro is a very wise man because of his speaking to Moses later on.

One day as Moses is tending his flocks, and he sees on Mt. Sinai a bush that is burning that continues to burn but never goes it. Sometimes, in the desert it gets so hot that it is normal that a bush may burn, but it always goes out. The bush he saw was burning but not consumed (Exodus 3). It got his attention so he walked up the mountain to see that bush. What happened is that God found a way to catch his attention. He climbed the mountain to get to the spot and that is where he met God.

Exodus 3: The angel of the Lord appeared to him in a flame of fire from the midst of a bush, and he looked, and the bush burned with fire, but the bush was not consumed. 3 So Moses said, "I will now turn aside and see this great sight, why the bush is not burnt."

4 When the Lord saw that he turned aside to see, God called to him from out of the midst of the bush and said, "Moses, Moses."

And he said, "Here am I."

5 He said, "Do not approach here. Remove your sandals from off your feet, for the place on which you are standing is holy ground." 6 Moreover He said, "I am the God of your father, the God of Abraham, the God of Isaac, and the God of Jacob." And Moses hid his face, for he was afraid to look upon God.

God speaks to Moses telling him that God has seen the abuse of his people Israel as slaves and has heard their cries. God gives instruction to Moses.

Exodus 3: 9 Now therefore, the cry of the children of Israel has come to Me. Moreover, I have also seen the oppression with which the Egyptians are oppressing them. 10 Come now therefore, and I will send you to Pharaoh so that you may bring forth My people, the children of Israel, out of Egypt."

God is choosing Moses as his representative or ambassador to request that Israel be set free from slavery. There is no way that Pharaoh who inherited the slaves for the last 400 years is going to give up the slaves because a person requests it. Egypt was not kind to the slaves; they had no respect for the slaves and certainly would not easily give them freedom.

Moses asks God to reveal His name because surely Pharaoh would want to know the name of the God asking that the slaves be set free.

Exodus 3: 14 And God said to Moses, "I AM WHO I AM,"[a] and He said, "You will say this to the children of Israel, 'I AM' has sent me to you.'"

The meaning of this "I AM WHO I AM" is that God always was, God always is, God will always be God – the one true God - the tetragrammaton (Jehovah translated into the King James Version as LORD). God instructs Moses to go speak to the children of Israel promising them that God will deliver them as He had promised. Also, he was to go and demand that Pharaoh let the slaves go free. Moses explains to God that he isn't a very good speaker and he doesn't believe he is the right person for the task (Exodus 4). God questions him by asking what is that in your hand? Moses had a shepherd's staff in his hand.

Exodus 4: 3 He said, "Throw it on the ground."

And he threw it on the ground, and it became a serpent. Then Moses fled from it. 4 Then the Lord said to Moses, "Put forth your hand and take it by the tail." And he put forth his hand, and caught it, and it became a rod in his hand. 5 "This is so that they may believe that the Lord, the God of their fathers, the God of Abraham, the God of Isaac, and the God of Jacob, has appeared to you."

6 The Lord said furthermore to him, "Now put your hand into your bosom." He put his hand into his bosom, and when he took it out, his hand was as leprous as snow.

7 He said, "Put your hand into your bosom again." So he put his hand into his bosom again and brought it out of his bosom, and it was restored like his other flesh.

8 "If they will not believe you, nor listen to the voice of the first sign, then they may believe the voice of the latter sign. 9 But if they will not believe also these two signs or listen to your voice, then you shall take water from the river and pour it on the dry land, and the water which you take out of the river will become blood on the dry land."

God gives him two demonstrations of God's power – the rod that can become a serpent and then become a rod again and his hand becoming leprous white and then returning normal again. He also instructs him that if Pharaoh will not believe, to place his rod in the water so that water taken of the Nile would become blood. Moses makes more excuses saying that he stutters and isn't a strong speaker. God explains to Moses that God created him and can do anything – including use Moses to do this mission; God is angry, but He is merciful towards Moses and says he can get his brother Aaron to help him.

Moses is a good man, a godly man but He does not have the Holy Spirit living in his heart. He is speaking with God directly but must make a leap of faith to believe what God is saying. If people are in bondage of any type, this was literal slavery for 400 years, people develop a slave mentality. It is hard for these people to think beyond their bondage. It is hard for them to imagine that God can do anything. God grew angry at Moses for his unbelief. Moses knows he himself cannot deliver the slaves but he doesn't even believe that God can use him to do it because he knew it was impossible to him. After God says that Aaron can help him, Moses is comforted somewhat.

Moses and Aaron present themselves to the Pharaoh and Moses says the following:

Exodus 5: 1 And afterward Moses and Aaron went in and said to Pharaoh, "Thus says the Lord, the God of Israel, 'Let My people go, that they may hold a feast to Me in the wilderness.' "

Pharaoh replies that he won't let the slaves go free. Moses throws his rod and the ground and it becomes a serpent. The Egyptian magicians did the same and their rods became serpents also, but Moses' serpent swallowed the other snakes and turned back into a rod again. Pharaoh becomes hardened in his heart and not only says that the slaves cannot be free, but also the Israelites could no longer use straw to make their bricks. The Israelites become angry and talked of killing Moses. Moses goes back to Sinai to speak to God on the mountain.

Exodus 6 Then the Lord said to Moses, "Now you shall see what I will do to Pharaoh, for with a strong hand shall he let them go, and with a strong hand shall he drive them out of his land."

God explains that He will manifest His glory through the deliverance of Israel out of Egypt. God explains that Pharaoh's heart is so hard that he will keep saying no but that God will show miraculous signs throughout Egypt so that God can be truly glorified for Israel's deliverance. God says that each time Pharaoh says no to God's demand, a plague will come on Egypt.

The plagues that came upon Egypt

Chapter 7: 14	Water turns to blood
Chapter 8 -	Plague of frogs
	Plague of gnats
	Plague of flies
Chapter 9:	Plague on livestock
	Boils
	Hail that turned into flame
Chapter 10	Locusts
	Darkness for three days
The final Plague	Death of the first born

God speaks with Moses and lets him know this is the final plague of the death of the first born. Egypt did not want to let Israel go free because they had them as slaves for 400 years and used them for many aspects of their labour. Also, Israel is God's chosen people. They were to inherit the promised land as God spoke to Abraham. The enemy of Israel does not want to let Israel go.

The final plague is that every first born would die unless Israel took lamb's blood and sprinkled it over the door posts and around the windows. It had to be a pure healthy lamb that was sacrificed.

Exodus 12: 5 Your lamb shall be without blemish, a male of the first year. You shall take it out from the sheep, or from the goats. 6 You shall keep it up until the fourteenth day of the same month, and then the whole assembly of the congregation of Israel shall kill it in the evening. 7 They shall take some of the blood and put it on the two side posts and on the upper doorpost of the houses in which they shall eat it. 8 They shall eat the flesh on that night, roasted with fire, and they shall eat it with unleavened bread and bitter herbs. 9 Do not eat it raw, nor boiled at all with water, but roasted with fire, its head with its legs and its entrails. 10 And you shall let nothing of it remain until the morning, but that of it which remains until the morning you shall burn with fire. 11 In this way shall you eat it: with your waist girded, your sandals on your feet, and your staff in your hand. So you shall eat it in haste. It is the Lord's Passover.

At about mid night the last plague came. Anyone who didn't have the lamb's blood over the door died. This happened all over Egypt including Pharaoh's first born son.

Exodus 12: 31 Then he called for Moses and Aaron at night and said, "Rise up, and get out from among my people, both you and the children of Israel, and go, serve the Lord, as you have said. 32 Also take your flocks and your herds, as you have said, and be gone, and bless me also."

Passover

That night gave God gave Moses special instruction concerning the Passover. God gives special instruction about the food. Their bread could have no leaven. Their lamb must be roasted. No uncircumcised person could eat of it. None could be saved for the next day. The bitter herbs are spoken of to remind them of their harsh life in slavery. The ordinance of the Passover celebration begins. Exodus 12: 43-50. Jewish people and Messianic Jewish people and some Christians celebrate this special day once a year to thank God for His delivering Israel out of Egypt.

When the angel of death came to the region, he saw the blood applied over the homes and passed over those places. If there was no blood applied, the first born of every home was slain. Jesus Christ fulfills this in the New Testament as His blood shed for us when he died on the cross. Faith in his blood gives us salvation, healing, deliverance. Jesus was without sin, pure as the spotless lamb that sacrificed. Jesus the Messiah is the Passover lamb. The prophet John the Baptist saw Jesus coming and proclaimed 'Behold the lamb of God who takes away the sin of the world (John 1: 29).

The Red Sea

Over 2, 000, 000 million Israelites left Egypt. As they were on their way, they got to the Red Sea, Pharaoh's heart gets hard again and he chases the Israelites. A pillar of flame separates the Egyptians from the Israelites. The Egyptian army is there to massacre Israel. Moses speaks to God and

God tells Moses to stretch his rod over the Red Sea. Moses obeys and the waves of the Red Sea parts so there is a pathway of dry ground through the midst of the Red Sea. The children of Israel pass through the midst of the Red Sea with all their herds and carts and people. The Egyptian army begins to chase Israel. As the last Israeli got on dry ground, God caused the heaps of water to cover the Egyptian army drowning them.

It must cause you to know the hardness of the Egyptians hearts that they saw the Red Sea part and still chased after the Israelites. They saw the miracles God did for Israel but they did not believe in God. That Red Sea coming crashing on the Egyptian army separated Israel from all that she had been for 400 years. The Red Sea was a turning point – as Israel was completely delivered from Egypt. Just as that Sea came crashing down, separating the Israelites from Egypt, if you truly believe in Jesus blood, you are cut off, separated from sin and hell and bondage. You are set free to worship God. God cuts off your old life.

Moses begins to lead the Israelites to Mt. Sinai. A cloud covered them as they passed through the wilderness to shade them and cover them. At night, a pillar of flame appeared to lead them and be light unto them. Moses and Miriam and the faithful Israelites praise God mightily for their salvation. There was a hardness in the Israeli`s hearts. Even though they had experienced deliverance by mighty miracles, they had enmity towards God. They doubted God. They demanded food and water. They talked of killing Moses.

God sent manna (Exodus 16); In Hebrew, it literally means "what is it". It was as bread but it was tiny grains like a coriander seed. It was used to bake bread. God would give it to them every day (except the Sabbath) for the next 40 years. If you have not heard the Keith Green song about "you want to go back to Egypt", please find it and listen to it. It shows you the type of things the Israelites were talking about how they wished they could go back to Egypt because of the good things they missed there. The people only had the miracles. They did not have God`s Word yet so they were very fleshly and carnal. Instead of asking in faith for God to provide food and water, they demanded in a carnal, unbelieving way.

God caused water to spring forth out of a rock. There was enough water to water all the water for all of them. In a different place they wanted meat (Exodus 16) and they said it with hatred. God set quail, so many that there was more than enough – they ate too much. They finally get to Mt. Sinai. This is the place where God gives Moses the Mosaic covenant – the commandments.

The Commandments

Moses brings Israel to Mt. Sinai as God instructed him to do. Moses goes up the mountain to speak with God. The people are in valley below. Exodus 19 God has given them freedom from slavery and lead them by providing for them supernaturally. God speaks with Moses.

Exodus 19: 9 The Lord said to Moses, "Indeed, I am going to come to you in a thick cloud, so that the people may hear when I speak with you and always believe in you." Then Moses told the words of the people to the Lord.

God is affirming to Moses that he has been chosen to be the leader of Israel. God gives special instructions so that none of the people should even touch Mt Sinai. God was clearly defining His authority and the people obeyed. The people still had a slave mentality and they had enmity against God. It was as though God could not do enough for them. They had a hardness in their hearts towards God. It had to be changed before they could inherit the promised land first promised to Abraham. now to Moses. The people of Israel were delivered from Egypt but they had hard heartedness towards God.

God gave the 10 commandments to Moses. God also warned Moses that the people were wicked and not obedient.

Exodus 20: 1
Now God spoke all these words, saying:

2 I am the Lord your God, who brought you out of the land of Egypt, out of the house of bondage.

3 You shall have no other gods before Me.

4 You shall not make for yourself any graven idol, or any likeness of anything that is in heaven above, or that is in the earth beneath, or that is in the water below the earth. 5 You shall not bow down to them or serve them; for I, the Lord your God, am a jealous God, visiting the iniquity of the fathers on the children to the third and fourth generation of them who hate Me, 6 and showing lovingkindness to thousands of them who love Me and keep My commandments.

7 You shall not take the name of the Lord your God in vain, for the Lord

will not hold guiltless anyone who takes His name in vain.

8 Remember the Sabbath day and keep it holy. 9 Six days you shall labor and do all your work, 10 but the seventh day is a Sabbath to the Lord your God. On it you shall not do any work, you, or your son, or your daughter, or your male servant, or your female servant, or your livestock, or your sojourner who is within your gates. 11 For in six days the Lord made heaven and earth, the sea, and all that is in them, and rested on the seventh day. Therefore the Lord blessed the Sabbath day and made it holy.

12 Honor your father and your mother, that your days may be long in the land which the Lord your God is giving you.

13 You shall not murder.

14 You shall not commit adultery.

15 You shall not steal.

16 You shall not bear false witness against your neighbor.

17 You shall not covet your neighbor's house; you shall not covet your neighbor's wife, or his manservant, or his maidservant, or his ox, or his donkey, or anything that is your neighbor's.

These commandments cover all of man's relationship with God and man's relationship with people. God's instructions were to bring life to those of Israel who would listen to the word of God and let it circumcise their hearts towards Him – literally cut away their hard hearts and reveal a soft heart that wanted to please God. I do teach on the commandments in a different teaching but I only summarize them here.

1. Have no other Gods – Worship only the one true God the "I AM"

2. Make no graven image – no idols. We are forbidden to worship statues or pictures.

3. Do not take the name of the LORD God in vain. This not only means no cursing using God's name but also, no foolish talking with God's name.

4. Keep the Sabbath Day – no work on that day. God commanded

us to rest on 1 day in every seven. This was not only to rest the animals and the people but so that we could worship God on that day without distraction.

The Sabbath was the Saturday. Christians usually celebrate on a Sunday and it is because Sunday was the day Jesus rose from the dead. It doesn't mean you cannot do anything on your Sunday - but the prioritizing of God is for us to honour God and reflect on Him and worship Him wholly at least one in seven days as a church family. If we do not give ourselves a rest period, there will be spiritual consequences, such as loss of relationship with God and physical health issues because of wearing out our bodies. God commanded us to rest and rejoice with our loved ones so that we might be strengthened and refreshed.

4. Honour your mother and father that you might live a long life. This is a blessing tagged on to the promise. In other words, if you do not honour your parents, you will not live a long live.

5. Do not murder. If someone murders, his or her life must end. This is to place a consequence on violence and to teach people right from wrong. The people of Sodom and Gomorrah were violent. The Israelites had been used and abused for 400 years. They needed the specifics of what was pleasing to God and what God hated.

6. Do not commit adultery. Sex outside of marriage is forbidden.

7. Do not steal. You cannot go without penalty for theft. Usually the thief would have to repay the debt 7X.

8. Do not bear false witness. No lying. Honesty is expected.

9. Do not covet. Do not lust after what is not yours. That includes people, animals or things. It is not wrong to like someone else's property but it is wrong to lust after it. Instead of lust or covetousness, we should pray and God will give us our own things. The sin is is wanting someone else's something. Part of a sin is not knowing that God can supply for you just as He did for that other person.

The Commandments

These are the 10 commandments that were given to Moses. In itself, the giving of the Decalogue shows us how God wants us to live our lives and we should be thankful for it. What happened is that God literally took His finger and wrote on the stone on the mountain. He carved out two large tablets with His hand writing on them and gave them to Moses to share with the people. The giving of the commandments in this way shows it is God's Word becoming engraved on tablets of stone – spirit manifesting in physical form.

These are not all the commandments God gave to Moses. In total there were 613 laws or commandments given so that the Levites, the priests chosen by God could teach them to the people. They cover all aspects of human life: behaviour, relationships, dealings of business, bloodshed, retribution, consequences of sin etc.

Our laws in Canada and the United States were based upon the laws of God. Our nations were first Christian nations keeping the rules of God first. I remember in the 19 70's we used to have signs in parks that stated " no playing baseball on Sundays". Stores never used to be open on Sundays. We were honouring the Sabbath day as a nation.

There were also commanded feasts that Israel should keep as a nation.

Exodus 23: 14 Three times in the year you must celebrate a feast to Me.

15 You shall observe the Feast of Unleavened Bread. For seven days you shall eat unleavened bread, as I commanded you, in the appointed time of the month Aviv, for in it you came out from Egypt.

No one shall appear before Me empty-handed.

16 You shall observe the Feast of Harvest, the first fruits of your labors, which you have sown in the field.
You shall observe the Feast of Ingathering at the end of the year, when you have gathered in the fruit of your labors from the field.

17 Three times in the year all your males shall appear before the Lord God.

God's relationship with Moses

God speaks with Moses

God gives Moses these commandments and those stone tablets with the condensed version – or the 10 commandments on them. He later gives him the plans to build the tabernacle of the LORD, so that God's presence could be with them. God spoke with Moses as with a friend. Please see Moses has a unique relationship with God. He honours God and gives his life to serve God and God speaks much with him concerning all aspects of human life. Moses obeyed and served God for most of his life.

I hate it when Moses disobeys God in what seems like a small thing and it disqualifies himself from ever entering the promised land. God had commanded Moses to sing to the rock in the wilderness and water would spring forth from it. In this demonstration, God could have taught the people how to praise God. Moses gets angry with the grumbling complaining people and hits the rock in direct disobedience to God. By this, he dishonours God at Mira bah. If he could have taught the people to sing to the rock, praise could have been released in those people that day, giving God glory. Because of his sin, Moses cannot enter the promised land. He gets to see it from a mountain but it is Joshua who will lead the people into the promised land.

At the Bottom of Mt. Sinai

While Moses is speaking with God in a most Holy experience of man communing with God, the people of Israel in the valley are living in wickedness. They grumble and complain about Moses being gone so long and there are people who can stir up the multitudes to wickedness such as Dathan. He got the people to force Aaron to make a gold statue so they could worship it. Aaron obeys. The people are worshipping the gods of Egypt and in sin and drunkenness and all manner of immorality. It is at this mountain where Holiness is revealed and evil is revealed. Moses hears a sound and first thinks it is a sign of war. Then he realizes it is the sound of sin. The words of God given to Moses forbid all the things that Israel is doing.

Aaron who was used by God to help Moses, was chosen to be a priest to God, was persuaded and forced by the people to make that golden calf. The people worshipped that golden calf after seeing that the "I AM" Jehovah had delivered them from Egypt and provided for them in the wilderness. Sin is hatred towards God. Moses becomes very angry when he sees Israel sinning against God and in his anger, he throws the commandments at the people and they break. The most Holy commandments written by God Himself are destroyed.

Dathan and the other evil leaders with hatred or enmity towards God question Moses and don't want to follow him. Those who were worshipping that golden calf and doing wickedness, that wanted to go back to Egypt rather than serve God were separated that day. Moses calls for those who are on the LORD's side to come towards him. Those who are against God do not come near Moses. The dividing line was drawn. The righteous people, the Levites and all who honoured God go towards Moses and Aaron. Those who do not go with Moses are swallowed live by the earth in flames and covered by an earth quake. Moses states that if he is speaking for God with the commandments, the earth will consume all those who do not believe. It occurs right after he says it.

This is one occasion of Israel disobeyed God. In other instances, plagues come on people who are grumbling and complaining against Moses. The Israelites had hard hearts towards God and Moses. Even though God had delivered them, there was an anger against God; only God Himself could purge this from them.

The Glow of God's Presence

When Moses came down from the mountain, there was a glow about him – it was the glory of God on him. People knew he had been with God because of the glow on Moses. Because of this Moses put a veil over his face so the people would not focus on Moses but on God. The commandments, God rewrote them and gave them to Moses. Israel was given these commandments to live by. They were not suggestions. They were commandments. God clearly declared His will towards people and how we should live our lives.

Enmity

At this point, I want you to consider your own self. If there is anything in you that wants to shake your fist at God in anger, you must come to God and pray for mercy to repent. If there some part of you that wants your own way, even though you know it is disobedience to God's commandments, you must make an altar. Present yourself to God and ask Him to grant you repentance. You can't even repent without God's help. If there is some stubborn, part of you that wants your way that is different than God's way, please offer yourself to God and ask Him to cut out the hardness of your heart. Only God can remove this hardness. The only hope for you is that God will circumcise your heart and cut out that hard heart and give you a pure heart that loves and lives for God.

The hardness of heart I am speaking of can be sin inherited or sin practiced by the person. It can occur because of blaming God for the death of a loved one or for a tragedy. It is hatred towards God that will separate a person from God. There will always be a part of that person that will not obey. There will always be a separation between those people and God. Jesus Christ died for our sins, so that we could be fully reconciled to God in covenant friendship relationship. God can take a hard heart and by a miracle of His presence remove the hardness and give you a heart of love and honour for God.

Someone with a chip on his or her shoulder that has a hardness that believes God owes him or her something is a person with enmity. A person who is quick to curse the name of God or to argue or to be violent is this type of person. Although I describe it as a hard heart, I'm not sure that is visual enough. Imagine that a heart is soft as the tissues in a human body. The heart is meant to be made of tissues and muscles and human cells. If there were a hard spot, like a stone placed in the heart, the heart would not be able to function properly. That part of the heart could not receive the nutrients of the body. That part of the heart could not be used to build up or strengthen the body.

It would be a foreign thing that would damage the body because blood and nutrients wouldn't be able to flow to that area of the heart. We must pray asking God to remove from us the heart of stone. People who consistently sin and do the same sins and later repent and ask for prayer – could have a hardness of iniquity – inherited sins from a family who continuously sinned in that area. What happens is it makes you hard towards God. Only God can help you. You do not have to live that way. The same blood of Jesus that died for your sins also died to restore us to God so we could love God with all our heart, soul, mind and strength.

If this is you, repent and believe on the LORD Jesus Christ. Receive Him as your Saviour and your LORD (Acts 2: 38). If you are a Christian but still have this hardness, Repent and be water baptized believing that God will circumcise your heart. Pray for it and believe it that once you rise from the waters of baptism, you will be renewed in your heart and in your mind. Keep saying I have been baptized into the death, burial and resurrection of Christ. My heart is renewed. There is no enmity in me.

Colossians 2: 11 In Him you were also circumcised with the circumcision made without hands, by putting off the body of the sins of the flesh, by the circumcision of Christ, 12 buried with Him in baptism, in which also you were raised with Him through the faith of the power of God, who has raised Him from the dead.

I have known people who have been transformed by knowing that God circumcised their hearts in Water Baptism. Yes; it is an outward sign of faith, but with faith it has an opportunity to separate that person unto God for all of life.

The law was given to teach us what sin is so we wouldn't do it. It was also given to show us the way to have God's blessing upon our lives. The law was not meant to only be on tablets of stone but to be written on the inward parts of our heart.

Jeremiah 31: 33 But this shall be the covenant that I will make with the house of Israel after those days, says the Lord:
I will put My law within them
    and write it in their hearts;
and I will be their God,
    and they shall be My people.
34 They shall teach no more every man his neighbor
    and every man his brother, saying, "Know the Lord,"
for they all shall know Me,
    from the least of them to the greatest of them,
    says the Lord,
for I will forgive their iniquity,
    and I will remember their sin no more.

All of the commandments were given to show Israel how to live their lives with blessing because they did not know how to live their lives outside of slavery. It was given to be a blessing to us not a burden. Those who love God will want to obey His commandments. Please know Jesus Christ did not destroy the laws of Moses or the Mosaic covenant. Instead He came to fulfill them. Jesus Christ never broke any laws. He kept them all with a perfect heart. He lived a Holy life so that He could die for our sins taking our place on the cross so that by faith in Him we could be set free from the curse of the law.

I talk of the commandments in a different teaching but I am asking you personally to examine your own heart. You know whether you have completely submitted your life to God or not. If there is a hardness, you do not have to live with it. You can live wholly, spirit soul and body given to God (1 Thessalonians 5: 23). If you have any negative feeling towards God it includes you.

Forgiveness

If you have any negative feelings towards a person, or yourself, you must forgive. No matter what a person has done to you, you must forgive. I am not talking about living in abuse or any type. God doesn't want any one abusing you verbally, physically or sexually. Get out of that atmosphere if you are in it. Once you are out of that atmosphere, you must pray and forgive that person. I am not saying you go back to it. I am saying you are commanded to forgive. Jesus Christ forgave us; He commands us to forgive others so that our sins might be forgiven also.

If we do not forgive, we will not be forgiven. This should be a strong motivator to forgive. You don't have to feel like forgiving. Do it as an act of obedience to God. Say it our loud. In the name of Jesus, I forgive so and so. Pray that there will be no root of bitterness in you (Hebrews 12: 15). If you have wronged a person in any way and God brings it to you, go to that person and ask for forgiveness. Pray thanking Jesus for washing your sins from you. Receive forgiveness as a gift from God. If you do not forgive others, you will not be forgiven. Let there be no strife in your life. The Israelites were constantly grumbling and complaining. They were living a carnal life. Live in the Spirit, not in the flesh.

If you have not heard Joyce Meyer telling her testimony, I highly recommend you get the teaching; she was raised in a very abusive home and God transformed her life and healed her and how God used her to not only forgive those people but to pray for them and to bless them and even buying them things they needed and giving them aide until her parents came to accept Jesus Christ as Saviour and LORD. She witnessed to them and showed them the love of God; their lives were transformed because of it.

God can completely heal you so even the remembrance of sin or abuse done to you can be seen from your position in Christ seated with Jesus in heavenly places (Ephesians 2: 6). God can remove the sting of what happened to you. God can completely heal and make you whole so there is no hardness in your heart and no bitterness towards God or people.

You roll the care of that sin against you onto God. You believe that Jesus can blot out any negative aspect of the sins against you (1 Peter 5: 7).

God knows what has been done to you. The Apostle Paul prays almost the exact prayer. He speaks to God of what Alexander the coppersmith had done to him and rolls the care of it onto Jesus asking Jesus to judge the matter:

2 Timothy 4: 14. Commit the matter to God. Let Jesus Christ care for that area of your life. Forgive and let no forgiveness be in you. If there is any hatred towards people for what they have done to you, repent and give the matter to God.

Jesus tells us to pray for those who abuse us. Why? Because if you are a servant of God, God Himself fights against those who fight against you. Your heart should be pure without bitterness or hatred. God Himself will defend you. Pray mercy on those people who fight against you knowing they are deceived or manipulated by the devil. Surely, they curse themselves by fighting against you.

If you have been to a Messianic Passover celebration, you will see a part of the service where the people pray for those who did them wrong and pray mercy on them knowing that God defends them and God may reveal Himself to them so they can be saved.

Justice

Sometimes in North America, we are not sure there will be justice by the legal system. It never used to be that way, but that`s how it is today. If you can get a slick talking lawyer who can find some wiggle room in the law or a loophole, a person such as a murderer or abuser can be set free. On occasions such as these, you will often see thousands of people protesting demanding Justice. People have an inner desire to see true justice done to those who murder or molest children or rape or do such terrible things.

God is not like our system. God is always just. We will always get justice from God. You may not see it, but God always deals with those who fight against others; evil doers will give answer to every sin they commit at the white Throne Judgement Seat. They will not escape. The evidence will be that God can point out specifically what they did and against whom them did it to. Please pray mercy for those people. Unless they repent, they cannot be saved.

Pray mercy for those who have abused or sinned against you because perhaps God will soften their hearts and they will change. Sin isn't the problem with them. Their desire to sin and do evil over their obedience to

God is their issue. They that willfully do evil will be judged. Pray they may repent before they are judged at the white Throne Judgement because once judged there – there is only the destiny of total separation from God for all of eternity. It is a horror. Pray for mercy that God will deal with them and grant them repentance.

Pray

Literally ask God to forgive you, for harboring bitterness or hatred to anyone. As you pray, say I roll the care of this thing done to me onto you. I plead the blood over me concerning it. There is no unforgiveness in me. Have mercy on that person so that he or she might find repentance. This doesn't mean there are not consequences. For example, if someone kills a member of your family, there is often hatred towards that person. Your family may want to kill that person. You must pray that God will deal with the situation. Pray for justice to be done, because he or she broke both the commandments and the law of the land.

In many countries if rape or murder were to happen, that murderer would die. In our countries, there is no capital punishment. There is some capital punishment in some of the United States but not all states. We must literally pray for God to care concerning that situation. It is not right for us to hold onto feelings of unforgiveness or bitterness even against murderers. God is a just God. You may believe that a person got free from the justice system of the earth because he or she did not go to jail; that may be true, but there is a Judgement Throne that no person can escape. The judgements from that throne are for all of eternity.

We who are the Christians, must be the standard bearers. We cannot let the standard fall. That means we forgive whether or not we feel like it. We must bear the standard of holiness. That means we remain right with God, a pure heart, giving and forgiving. God is the judge (Romans 12: 19); He will always fight against those who fight against you.

In Deuteronomy 11, 28, 30, The blessings and consequences of God dealing with people who obey or disobey God are given to Moses concerning all types of ways God will bless the people of the Mosaic Covenant. It means keeping the laws given to Moses and living lives following after God.

Deuteronomy 28: 3 The Lord will establish you as a holy people to Himself, just as He swore to you, if you will keep the commandments of the Lord your God and walk in His ways. 10 All people of the earth shall see that you are called by the name of the Lord, and they shall be afraid of you. 11 The Lord will make you overflow in prosperity, in the offspring of your body, in the offspring of your livestock, and in the produce of your ground, in the land which the Lord swore to your fathers to give you.

God promises blessings over every part of a human life including health, prosperity, blessings on children and animals and all manner of work etc. God's got blessings in those scriptures I've quoted that cover every area of human life. Please see the law was given to be how God could be honoured by people so that God could bless and prosper us.

The Standard of Forgiveness

The only standard we should use to compare ourselves to is Jesus standard. As he was physically beaten until his flesh was all bleeding and the nails were pounded through His hands and feet, a crown of thorns piercing his head, blood streaming down, in his dying moments he prayed for us.

Luke 23: 34 Jesus said, "Father, forgive them, for they know not what they do." And they divided His clothes by casting lots.

He was praying for those who abused him. He was praying for you and I. He was praying for all people who had ever lived, that He might bear all the sins of the world that should we believe in Christ, we could be saved. Any lower standard of forgives is not acceptable.

What if you Can t Forgive

Don't say 'I cannot forgive.' Yes you can. Start saying it before you feel like saying it - by faith. Say 'I forgive them. O God I need your forgiveness so God I forgive them.' Keep saying it until it gets down on the innermost part of your being. Say it by faith expecting Jesus to renew you. Correct yourself with your own mouth. Say it out loud I forgive by faith. Jesus cares for that situation.

Joyce Meyer

Joyce Meyer talks about forgiving by faith and then praying a blessing over the person who sinned against you. She also talks of how God moves her to give to those people something of a blessing – such as a gift. She has no bitterness or unforgiveness in her heart because she chooses to do it God's way. God's way is that He will fight against those who come to you.

`You may not think famous people have much opposition. That isn`t true. There are people who because of covetousness or jealousy or hatred will spread gossip about you or lies about you. They will attack a person for no reason. Don`t stay in the company of someone who has a critical spirit. If the person is always angry about someone or something, the person has got enmity issues; hatred in his or her heart. The person is not good company. What you tolerate in your life, you may start doing. The person should be warned about his or her sin. If the person doesn't repent, separate yourself from that person`s influence. That person can only pollute your life with bitterness.

If you hang on to unforgiveness, it becomes a hard spot in your heart separating you from God and separating you from the blessings of God`s covenant with us. It can block answers to prayer; it can manifest itself in physical ailments. It can stop a person from receiving God`s best for their lives. I don`t want anything separating me from God. Forgive because you know you want God more than anything else and you obey His commandment to forgive.

Bitterness or resentment against others is as a terrible type of spiritual cancer that will contaminate you and cause hard spots in your heart. That means it is most certain you will be against God. I cannot explain to you how much I need forgiveness from God 24/7 - 365. I don't want to be separated from God. I want God more than anything on earth. Confess it your own self. Make it your confession if someone sins against you. A sinner who sins against you is going to hell if he or she does not repent. Pray mercy on the person because the person is judged already by God`s word. Those who fight against you, God will fight against.

Prayer

O God if there is any enmity in our hearts, you would quicken to us so we could repent and focus on God. God let me desire your commandments as much as I desire life. Let me honour your Word above all. Thank you for the Covenant you made with Moses. Thank you that Jesus lives in me and through the empowering presence of the Holy Spirit I can live in freedom with no sin or unforgiveness. I release any who have sinned against me. God have mercy on them that they might repent. Amen.

End of Chapter Questions

1. Describe your interpretation of the commandments. What does God require?
2. How can you keep the commandments?
3. If the is some person you have not forgiven, say it with your mouth out loud that you forgive the person. Pray asking God to bring conviction to the person so the person can repent.

5 THE NEW COVENANT

The New Covenant

The promise of the Messiah in the scriptures, the one who would come redeem us from the curse of Adam began in Genesis 3: 15. In truth the scriptures tell us that Jesus was slain from the foundations of the earth because God knew what we would do and provided a sacrifice. In the midst of giving the curses of sin upon the serpent, the man and the woman, God promised that one born of woman would crush the serpent's head. This did not only mean the physical animal but the devil also. Throughout the other chapters of this book, we see attempting to connect with man through various covenants. The people had a part to fulfill and God made certain promises. None of the covenants have been revoked.

The Covenants

God's promises to Adam and Eve to populate the earth are true to us today. But the promise their covenant had, in the Messiah coming to redeem fallen man has been accomplished in the birth, life, death and resurrection of Jesus Christ. God's promise to Noah that they should repopulate the earth is still God's desire for us today. The rainbow in the sky, usually after a rain, is a constant reminder to us that God promised never to destroy all of the earth, all of the people or all of the animals ever again. The rainbow should cause us to remember that God keeps His Word.

Also true, God's promise to Abraham to make of him mighty nations and that kings would be born of him and that his people would inherit the promised land and that they would be blessed because God would bless those who blessed them and curse those who cursed them. After thousands of years, Israel exists with the same language that was used for thousands of years. That would be significant evidence of God's faithfulness in itself, but the scattering of Israel and destruction of it by her enemies – to the complete restoration and rebuilding of the nation of Israel is a miracle only God could do. This gives us hope for the prophecies about Israel that yet have to be fulfilled.

The blessings of the covenants that God made with these people are important today to show us God's will towards us and His desire to bless us. The Mosaic laws were not made void by the coming of Jesus Christ.; rather, Jesus kept them all so fulfilled them – He is our righteousness.

Please see that Jesus came to fulfill the laws and the prophecies about the Messiah; He did not destroy the covenants, but He fulfilled them completely. The chances of a person completely fulfilling all the laws of Moses and all the prophetic scriptures about the Messiah are impossible if Jesus Christ were not God. Please see a summary of the covenants God made with humans.

The Covenants: The requirements

Adam -   God commanded Adam and Eve to populate the earth, give animal sacrifice for their sins.

Noah-   God commanded Noah to repopulate the earth; God promised people and animals, the earth would remain; the rainbow is a symbol of this covenant. Animal sacrifices covered sins people.

Abraham God promised from Abraham would be a mighty nation; promise of a seed (lineage) too numerous to count as stars of sky. Prosperity, was promised. Animal sacrifice was given for sins of people. Circumcision of all males was a sign of the covenant.

Moses   Moses was given the commandments of God. God clearly instructs Moses so he could give Israel His Word – so that blessings would be on them to live long, prosperous, healthy, with strength. Animal sacrifice was made for sins of people by the Levitical priests.

The New Covenant – Jesus Christ the Messiah

The New Covenant Jesus kept all the laws of Moses, so he fulfilled all the promises of the Messiah, took upon Himself all sins of the world so that there is no longer need for animal sacrifice. Humans can be totally reconciled to God.

Accepting Jesus as Saviour, leads to the indwelling of the Holy Spirit, the gifts of the Spirit, the blessings of all the previous covenants through faith in Jesus Christ. We have the hope of Christ's return to rule and reign. We are promised eternal life.

Through the covenants, God showed us His immeasurable love towards us and His desire to bless us and to have relationship with us.

Jesus Christ is the Messiah

Jesus Christ was born as was prophesied in the Old Testament; he was conceived of the Virgin Mary while she was promised to Joseph as his fiancée. Jesus Christ had supernatural aspects concerning his birth. Angels ministered to Mary, to Joseph, and to shepherds. Kings from other nations came to worship the Christ because of the unusual star in the sky that marked the place of his birth. He was prophesied over as a baby as he was dedicated in the temple by both Simeon a prophet and Anna a prophetess. His name was given by God. He lived an ordinary life in the home of believers; he had natural brothers and sisters from what we know in the Bible. If it were important for us to know about Jesus' life from ages 12 – 30, God would have included it in the scriptures.

Jesus is God

It was not until Jesus was 30 years old that he was introduced as a teacher and proclaimed the Messiah by John the Baptist who said Jesus is as the lamb of God who came to take away the sins of the world (John 1: 29). It is at the age of thirty, that Jesus began his public ministry. Throughout the Bible, Jesus was called divine names. Never once did he deny it. He corrected people if they made errors about him. The strongest statement came from Thomas who doubted that Jesus had risen from the dead until he saw him face to face.

John 20: But he said to them, "Unless I see the nail marks in his hands and put my finger where the nails were, and put my hand into his side, I will not believe."

26 A week later his disciples were in the house again, and Thomas was with them. Though the doors were locked, Jesus came and stood among them and said, "Peace be with you!" 27 Then he said to Thomas, "Put your finger here; see my hands. Reach out your hand and put it into my side. Stop doubting and believe."

28 Thomas said to him, "My Lord and my God!"

29 Then Jesus told him, "Because you have seen me, you have believed; blessed are those who have not seen and yet have believed."

Jesus is God

Jesus blesses Thomas by saying he believed because he saw proof. He also said more blessed are those who believe but haven't seen Him. Jesus Himself proclaimed to be one with God (John 14: 9). Jesus stated that he was the "I AM" (John 18:5)

Jesus had no father but God. Joseph raised Jesus but God placed Jesus in Mary's virgin womb. What this means is that sins and iniquities passed on through the father's blood line did not get passed on to Jesus. Jesus had no sin. Jesus had no sin of Adam in his heritage. His heritage came through his mother and through all of the prophetic words about the Messiah. He is a descendent of king David as was promised to David by God (2 Samuel 7 : 5- 16). The prophetic fulfillment of the Word of God is His inheritance. They are proofs that He is God's Son – equal with God – God living in human form.

John 1: 1 In the beginning was the Word, and the Word was with God, and the Word was God. 2 He was with God in the beginning. 3 Through him all things were made; without him nothing was made that has been made. 4 In him was life, and that life was the light of all mankind. 5 The light shines in the darkness, and the darkness has not overcome[a] it.

1 John 5: 20 We know also that the Son of God has come and has given us understanding, so that we may know him who is true. And we are in him who is true by being in his Son Jesus Christ. He is the true God and eternal life.

When Jesus was baptized by John the Baptist in the Jordan River, a voice came booming from Heaven. It was God saying that Jesus was his beloved son in whom he was pleased) Matthew 3: 17) also there appeared like a dove above his head and John the Baptist identified it as a sign of the Messiah.

Jesus' Ministry Displayed God's Authority

While on the earth, as a human man, Jesus ministry is known for the miracles, healings, and other supernatural demonstrations of His authority. He travelled throughout the region preaching the good news of forgiveness of sins, healing, and deliverance. Miracles followed his preaching. The gospels are written so that we might know what Jesus did in his earthly ministry.

John 20: 30 Jesus performed many other signs in the presence of his disciples, which are not recorded in this book. 31 But these are written that you may believe[b] that Jesus is the Messiah, the Son of God, and that by believing you may have life in his name.

John 21: 24 This is the disciple who testifies to these things and who wrote them down. We know that his testimony is true.

25 Jesus did many other things as well. If every one of them were written down, I suppose that even the whole world would not have room for the books that would be written.

Mark 2: 'Get up, take your mat and walk'? 10 But I want you to know that the Son of Man has authority on earth to forgive sins." So he said to the man, 11 "I tell you, get up, take your mat and go home." 12 He got up, took his mat and walked out in full view of them all. This amazed everyone and they praised God, saying, "We have never seen anything like this!"

Jesus was truly a Human

Jesus was born of a woman. He had a human body. He could feel the way we feel. He grew from a baby to a man. His mother and Joseph loved him and cared for him. He had brothers and sisters. God confined Himself on the earth to living as a human with the anointing of the Holy Spirit. He was trained by Joseph to be a carpenter. He had natural talents and skills as any person.

He attended the synagogue regularly and studied the scriptures because he knew the scriptures and was called to read as was the custom of those who regularly attended. The first years of his life were important because he knows what it is to live a human life and to see it through a human's eyes. This may seem obvious to us – but to Almighty God who created all things. Who is all knowing, all wise, omnipotent, omniscient, and omnipresent – he sacrificed much to become as one of us.

He lived a holy life. He did not sin. He did not break the commandments. Jesus never had to give an animal sacrifice for his sins because he was without sin. He lived holy. He was tempted, yet without sin (Hebrews 4: 15).

The Disciples

One of the first parts of his ministry was that he gathered to his disciples. They were ordinary people: fishermen, a tax collector – ordinary labourers. He revealed Himself as God through His friendship with them and through him discipline them and teaching them and using them to do miracles and preach the good news that Messiah had come. He started with 12.

Mark 3: 14 He appointed twelve[a] that they might be with him and that he might send them out to preach 15 and to have authority to drive out demons. 16 These are the twelve he appointed: Simon (to whom he gave the name Peter), 17 James son of Zebedee and his brother John (to them he gave the name Boanerges, which means "sons of thunder"), 18 Andrew, Philip, Bartholomew, Matthew, Thomas, James son of Alphaeus, Thaddaeus, Simon the Zealot 19 and Judas Iscariot, who betrayed him.

Next There Were 72

Luke 10: 1 After this the Lord appointed seventy-two[a] others and sent them two by two ahead of him to every town and place where he was about to go. 2 He told them, "The harvest is plentiful, but the workers are few. Ask the Lord of the harvest, therefore, to send out workers into his harvest field."

After the resurrection, as Jesus is visibly ascending up into heaven, about 500 people saw Him rise into the heavens and angels fill the skies.

More than 500 Witnesses

1 Corinthians 15: 6 After that, he appeared to more than five hundred of the brothers and sisters at the same time, most of whom are still living, though some have fallen asleep. 7 Then he appeared to James, then to all the apostles, 8 and last of all he appeared to me also, as to one abnormally born.

Jesus also appeared in person to the apostle Paul. Jesus has appeared to many people since His resurrection, including John who wrote the book of Revelation. There are documented proofs within the scriptures of his resurrection. He stayed on the earth forty days before ascending up into heaven.

Jesus the Messiah

Believing in Jesus Christ as Messiah Saviour is the only way to be reconciled to God. No other way is possible. Jesus proclaimed I Am the way, the truth and the life (John 14: 6). In the three years of Jesus' ministry, he impacted the earth more than any other person. What He did through his teachings and the demonstration of his authority over sin, sickness, evil and death itself, showed to all that He is God. He fulfilled the prophecies of the Old Testament Prophecies about the Messiah. Because he lived without sin, he alone is holy. Because he freely offered himself to atone for or take the consequences for all sins of all people, he is our Saviour. Only God could meet the requirement to pay the penalty of Adam's sin against God. Jesus gave His life willingly. He died on the cross that any who would believe that He is the Son of God would have eternal life.

Isaiah 53: 4 Surely he took up our pain
   and bore our suffering,
yet we considered him punished by God,
   stricken by him, and afflicted.
5 But he was pierced for our transgressions,
   he was crushed for our iniquities;
the punishment that brought us peace was on him,
   and by his wounds we are healed.
6 We all, like sheep, have gone astray,
   each of us has turned to our own way;
and the Lord has laid on him
   the iniquity of us all.

John 10:17 The reason my Father loves me is that I lay down my life—only to take it up again. 18 No one takes it from me, but I lay it down of my own accord. I have authority to lay it down and authority to take it up again. This command I received from my Father."

Jesus the Lamb of God

Jesus offered himself as a lamb without blemish had been offered to atone for sin according to the instructions God gave to Moses. If a person sinned, he or she must offer a sheep or goat as a sin offering. He or she would bring the animal to the Temple and the priests would offer the sacrifice. The sacrifice of animals covered the sins until Messiah would come. It was not erased but it was covered – waiting for the full forgiveness of sin through the promised Messiah. Jesus is the Messiah. He died and rose from the dead on the third day as he said he would do. Please don't believe because he knew he would rise from the dead made it any easier to die on the cross.

Isaiah 53: 10 Yet it was the Lord's will to crush him and cause him to suffer, and though the Lord makes[c] his life an offering for sin,
he will see his offspring and prolong his days,
   and the will of the Lord will prosper in his hand.

He knew excruciating pain as he was whipped and beaten and as huge nails were pounded through his hands and feet. He was crucified. The horror of all was that all sin that had ever existed, was placed on him. He willingly took it so that man could be redeemed. The reality of the pain gave him the authority to die for you or for me. He died as a human man. His spirit left his physical body. He was buried. There is a physical tomb that people visit as a holy site. He completely identified with humans in his birth and life and death. He triumphed over death, defeating the devil because Jesus was the ransom or the payment for all the sins that came into the earth because of Adam and Eve. Jesus rose from the dead on the third day and appeared to his disciples for 40 days before ascending up into heaven.

The Foundations of the New Covenant

Forgiveness from All Sin and Iniquity

Instead of simply atoning for man's sin – or covering it – as the animal sacrifices had done, Jesus blood shed for us erases our sins as though they never existed. Faith in Jesus Christ and in His blood cleanses us, frees us, gives us access to God. The covenant God made with us through the life, death, resurrection of Jesus Christ was unilateral. He paid for any sin ever committed including the sin of Adam and Eve. It gives the believer total right standing with God or the freedom to live holy. He not only provided the blessings of the covenant but He also paid the price Himself for it.

1 John 1: 7 But if we walk in the light, as he is in the light, we have fellowship with one another, and the blood of Jesus, his Son, purifies us from all[b] sin.

Relationship with God

Not only can believers talk to God but by the miracle of the new birth (John 3: 3) the Holy Spirit comes to live inside of us. Jesus gave us the Holy Spirit living inside of our spirit so we are never without God's presence. God lives in Christians. His Holy Spirit fills our human spirits. He literally breathed on the disciples to impart the Holy Spirit.

John 20: 21 Again Jesus said, "Peace be with you! As the Father has sent me, I am sending you." 22 And with that he breathed on them and said, "Receive the Holy Spirit. 23 If you forgive anyone's sins, their sins are forgiven; if you do not forgive them, they are not forgiven."

Jesus promised He would live inside of us.

John 14: 23 Jesus replied, "Anyone who loves me will obey my teaching. My Father will love them, and we will come to them and make our home with them. 24 Anyone who does not love me will not obey my teaching. These words you hear are not my own; they belong to the Father who sent me.

He promised not only the disciples but anyone who would believe on him that they could be filled with the Holy Spirit. He speaks this through the disciple Peter on the day of Pentecost.

Acts 2: 38 Peter replied, "Repent and be baptized, every one of you, in the name of Jesus Christ for the forgiveness of your sins. And you will receive the gift of the Holy Spirit. 39 The promise is for you and your children and for all who are far off—for all whom the Lord our God will call."

The Indwelling of the Holy Spirit

The indwelling of the Holy Spirit is total reconciliation with God. It surpasses any relationship God has ever had with man through covenant. Throughout the Old Testament, God's Spirit would come rest upon a person and he or she would prophesy or be used of God to do miracles such as the Prophetess Deborah or the Prophet Elijah or Elisha. Often prophets would either play an instrument or travel with someone who did worship God. They did not have the constant abiding presence of God with them. God inhabits the praises of His people. As they praised God, the glory of God would be evident in their midst and the Holy Spirit would move on the prophets to prophesy.

In matters of war, the ark of the covenant and the presence of God in it and the Levitical priests would lead the army into Battle. The strongest aspect of Israel is God's glory in her midst. God fought for Israel.

Numbers 31: 6 Moses sent them into battle, a thousand from each tribe, along with Phinehas son of Eleazar, the priest, who took with him articles from the sanctuary and the trumpets for signaling.

God's presence gave Israel victory over her enemies. This is evident with Moses on the way to the promised land and Joshua as Israel claims the promised land. As Christians, God's Holy presence is always with us. We can know God in a unique way because of His teaching us, leading us, guiding us, correcting us, etc. all from within our human spirits. This is the glory the Apostle Paul is talking about when he says we have this glory in earthen vessels (2 Corinthians 4: 7)

Spiritual Gifts

As if it were not enough to have total communion with God so that He can talk with us and we can talk to Him because He lives in our spirits, He also gives us Spiritual gifts. The emphasis on this comes after the day of Pentecost when God poured out his spirit to fulfill Joel 2:28.

Acts 2: 1 When the day of Pentecost came, they were all together in one place. 2 Suddenly a sound like the blowing of a violent wind came from heaven and filled the whole house where they were sitting. 3 They saw what seemed to be tongues of fire that separated and came to rest on each of them. 4 All of them were filled with the Holy Spirit and began to speak in other tongues[a] as the Spirit enabled them.

The 120 disciples who gathered in the upper room were in obedience to Jesus who instructed them to go wait in Jerusalem until they were empowered by the Holy Spirit. The Holy Spirit baptism is for men and women, and children and all who are Christians believing that Jesus died for our sins and rose again. The baptism of the Holy Spirit is an initial evidence of the infilling of the Holy Spirit with speaking in tongues but there are manifestations of the gifts of the Spirit to empower us to teach and preach Christ.

1 Corinthians 12: 7 Now to each one the manifestation of the Spirit is given for the common good. 8 To one there is given through the Spirit a message of wisdom, to another a message of knowledge by means of the same Spirit, 9 to another faith by the same Spirit, to another gifts of healing by that one Spirit, 10 to another miraculous powers, to another prophecy, to another distinguishing between spirits, to another speaking in different kinds of tongues,[a] and to still another the interpretation of tongues.[b] 11 All these are the work of one and the same Spirit, and he distributes them to each one, just as he determines.

These gifts make it possible for us to effectively talk about Jesus and teach the scriptures to people. God can use us through these gifts to bring salvation, healing and deliverance to people in the name of Jesus Christ. God used the early Christian church with these gifts but He also can use you or I also. The gifts of the spirit are for the Church to use to preach the gospel.

The Great Commission: Jesus Saves

Jesus made it clear to his disciples what they were to do after he had risen from the dead. He spoke to them commanding them to preach the good news. The good news is that Messiah has come. Jesus has reconciled man to God. Jesus is our Saviour. Jesus is alive. Jesus is living in His Church. Jesus can and does manifest His glory in and through believers. We are to continue the work of Jesus Christ on the earth. That includes sharing their sins can be forgiven. They can be healed; they can be set free; they can know a peace beyond all earthly knowledge. They can be one with God.

Mark 16: 15 He said to them, "Go into all the world and preach the gospel to all creation. 16 Whoever believes and is baptized will be saved, but whoever does not believe will be condemned. 17 And these signs will accompany those who believe: In my name, they will drive out demons; they will speak in new tongues; 18 they will pick up snakes with their hands; and when they drink deadly poison, it will not hurt them at all; they will place their hands on sick people, and they will get well."

19 After the Lord Jesus had spoken to them, he was taken up into heaven and he sat at the right hand of God. 20 Then the disciples went out and preached everywhere, and the Lord worked with them and confirmed his word by the signs that accompanied it.

Where the gospel is preached with passion, there is evidence of Jesus Christ living in the midst of those people. Jesus saves! By believing in your heart and confessing with your mouth that Jesus Christ is LORD you are saved (Romans 10: 9). We can live holy – by giving ourselves unto God wholly, spirit, soul and body as a free will offering to God (1 Thessalonians 5: 23) . Not only can we be forgiven of sin, we can live in the Spirit so there is no attraction to sin and no more remembrance of it or desire for it.

Hebrew 9: 14 How much more, then, will the blood of Christ, who through the eternal Spirit offered himself unblemished to God, cleanse our consciences from acts that lead to death, [c] so that we may serve the living God!

Jesus Delivers

Jesus not only died so that we could be forgiven; He redeems us from the curse of sin. We no longer desire it or want it. It is possible for a Christian to live holy; live in the Spirit. If we sin, we immediately repent and thank God for His blood that redeems us. We no longer have to be addicted to sin. This is news worth shouting about! Most people believe that even though you believe in God, well you have some dirty old sin habits and you just have to keep repenting for them. The good news is Jesus delivers us from all bondage. We do not have to be addicted to anything whether it is drugs or alcohol or sex or pornography or any such thing!

John 8: 34 Jesus replied, "Very truly I tell you, everyone who sins is a slave to sin. 35 Now a slave has no permanent place in the family, but a son belongs to it forever. 36 So if the Son sets you free, you will be free indeed.

Jesus Heals

Isaiah 53: But he was pierced for our transgressions,
    he was crushed for our iniquities;
the punishment that brought us peace was on him,
    and by his wounds we are healed.

Acts 3: 6 Then Peter said, "Silver or gold I do not have, but what I do have I give you. In the name of Jesus Christ of Nazareth, walk." 7 Taking him by the right hand, he helped him up, and instantly the man's feet and ankles became strong. 8 He jumped to his feet and began to walk. Then he went with them into the temple courts, walking and jumping, and praising God.

There is healing in the name of Jesus. You can pray for yourself to be healed. If you are a Christian, one of the signs of being a Christian is that people should be getting healed because of you. You should be praying for people to be healed. There are special meetings or church services where elders and pastors should pray for the sick and anoint them with oil and pray for healing. There is no disease that God cannot or will not heal.

Without faith, it is impossible to please God. (Hebrews 11:6). God manifests his glory when people believe in Him. The person praying must have faith in Jesus to heal. The person believing may not have faith of his or her own. That person should get a minister or elder to pray for him or her. That person could send prayer requests to reputable ministries believing they can pray in faith. You don't even have to be a Christian to be healed. Sometimes healings cause non - Christians to become Christians. Often someone's healing or miracle causes many people to believe because they knew the person before the healing, and are witnesses of the healing so they believe.

Personal Witness

I have been in many churches with the moving of God so strong by the Holy Spirit moving through the Church in the gifts of the Spirit. That I could barely stand without my knees shaking and buckling; I had to sit or kneel or lie prostrate. I have been in Evangelistic Crusade meetings and witnessed the healings and miracles all around me almost like popcorn popping so prevalent all around me in a crowd of more than twenty thousand people. I have seen my own friend completely delivered from smoking at such a meeting. I myself have completely received healing more than several occasions.

I say these things not to boast in my own self. I have received much teaching and instruction and mercy from God. I have known the presence of God so strong that my human body could not contain it. God is real. The same God who created all things, the same God who formed the heavens and the earth, the same God who made covenant with Adam and Eve is the same God who is God. He revealed Himself throughout the centuries to faithful men and women. He reveals Himself to us who will believe on the Lord Jesus Christ.

The Requirement of the New Covenant

The New Covenant that Jesus brought to us has only one requirement on our part: faith. We can only be saved by faith in Jesus Christ. We can only be saved or healed or delivered, by faith in Jesus Christ. Man, can only receive anything from God by faith.

Some may feel that they do not have this important factor of faith and are therefore excluded. No. The good news is that faith can come. It comes by hearing and by hearing God's Word (Romans 10: 17). What that means is if you do not have faith, press into someone who does have it. Go to a Church where they preach that the Bible is truly God's Word and that it applies to our lives in the present. You must invest in yourself to build your faith. Listening to strong faith teaching and preaching will help quicken your faith.

Christian Media

Christian Media can encourage you and inspire faith in your spirit. Christian media has been a significant influence in my life because I was the only Christian in my family. I only had one family of Christian friends in my early years as a Christian. Most of my fellowship or Christian companionship came through television preachers and teachers. I thank God for Trinity Broadcasting Network, a 24/7 Satellite network of stations, that broadcasts teachers and preachers, Christian movies, Christian documentaries, Christian World News, Christian entertainment, worship and praise. Preachers such as Kenneth and Gloria Copeland and Joyce Meyer and Marilyn Hickey and Benny Hinn were some of the most precious teachers in my life. I watched them on television and took notes as they preached. I would read and reread their books. I learned from them. When they came anywhere near my home, I made an effort to go to their conferences or events. I would buy their cd's and tapes and play them over and over again until the words got deep down in the inside of me. I soaked in as much word as I could possibly get. I recommend that you listen to any of these preachers or others who build your faith.

Faith Required

If you have a true need for faith, listening to preachers, such as mentioned, preach will inject raw potent faith directly into your spirit giving you faith to believe. It will give you faith to receive from God. Remember that in Mark 9: 23-25 Jesus does not condemn the man who wants faith that his son may be healed. The man cries out for healing of his son.

Mark 9: 21 Jesus asked the boy's father, "How long has he been like this?"

"From childhood," he answered. 22 "It has often thrown him into fire or water to kill him. But if you can do anything, take pity on us and help us."

23 "'If you can'?" said Jesus. "Everything is possible for one who believes."

24 Immediately the boy's father exclaimed, "I do believe; help me overcome my unbelief!"

All things are Possible

Jesus tells the man, if you can believe, all things are possible. The man immediately repents for his unbelief and begs Jesus to forgive him. Jesus is merciful. He answered the man's prayer and delivers his son and heals him. What does that mean to you or I? It means you must feed your faith just as you require food for nutrients, you need the Word of God for faith. It means you must get the Word of God into your ears. Hear the Word. It means you must get the Word of God into your heart: read the Word. It means you must get the Word of God into your spirit; meditate on the Word of God – speak it to yourself out loud so your own ears can hear it;

pray it over yourself; it is the engrafted word that is able to save the soul (James 1: 21).

Put the Word of God First

Faith comes by hearing and hearing comes through the Word of God. As you believe that Jesus saved you, so must you believe for healing or miracles. Jesus is the same God yesterday, today and forever (Hebrews 13:8). Since Faith is a direct result of reading God's Word, studying God's Word and hearing God's Word, it is essential that the Bible become a major part of your life.

The Blessings of the New Covenant

There are many aspects of the blessings of receiving Jesus Christ as Saviour. I only include some here. Accepting the New Covenant gives us eternal life with God.

Knowing that you have been forgiven for all sins through the blood of Jesus Christ gives us confidence to speak with God because He is our righteousness. He is our peace.

Acts 3: 38 "Therefore, my friends, I want you to know that through Jesus the forgiveness of sins is proclaimed to you. 39 Through him everyone who believes is set free from every sin, a justification you were not able to obtain under the law of Moses.

Being in communion with God knowing He not only hears and answers our prayers but wants to speak with us in intimate relationship is truly the primary blessing of the New Covenant. We can pray without ceasing because God lives on the inside of us.

1 Thessalonians 5: 16 Rejoice always, 17 pray continually, 18 give thanks in all circumstances; for this is God's will for you in Christ Jesus

Knowing true Christian friendship is stronger than any natural friendship could be, because Jesus is always in the midst of our relationships and helps to sharpen us and develop us spiritually. Jesus presence is always in the midst of our friendship.

Proverbs 27: 17 As iron sharpens iron,
    so one person sharpens another.

Matthew 18: 19 "Again, truly I tell you that if two of you on earth agree about anything they ask for, it will be done for them by my Father in heaven. 20 For where two or three gather in my name, there am I with them."

Long Life and Health

God wants us to care for our natural bodies and He promises long life and strength to those who honour Him. He promises to protect and deliver us.

Psalm 91: 4 "Because he[b] loves me," says the Lord, "I will rescue him;
I will protect him, for he acknowledges my name.
15 He will call on me, and I will answer him;
I will be with him in trouble,
I will deliver him and honor him.
16 With long life I will satisfy him
and show him my salvation."

Financial Prosperity

It is God's delight to see His people prospering financially. This was a promise to Abraham and to Isaac and to Jacob/Israel. It was a promise as part of the commandments given to Moses. God promises to bless us with talents and skills; God promises us fruitfulness; God promises us fertility; God promises us financial abundance.

Deuteronomy 28: 8 The Lord will send a blessing on your barns and on everything you put your hand to. The Lord your God will bless you in the land he is giving you.

9 The Lord will establish you as his holy people, as he promised you on oath, if you keep the commands of the Lord your God and walk in obedience to him. 10 Then all the peoples on earth will see that you are called by the name of the Lord, and they will fear you. 11 The Lord will grant you abundant prosperity—in the fruit of your womb, the young of your livestock and the crops of your ground—in the land he swore to your ancestors to give you.

12 The Lord will open the heavens, the storehouse of his bounty, to send rain on your land in season and to bless all the work of your hands. You will lend to many nations but will borrow from none. 13 The Lord will make you the head, not the tail. If you pay attention to the commands of

the Lord your God that I give you this day and carefully follow them, you will always be at the top, never at the bottom. 14 Do not turn aside from any of the commands I give you today, to the right or to the left, following other gods and serving them.

Deuteronomy 8: 18 But remember the Lord your God, for it is he who gives you the ability to produce wealth, and so confirms his covenant, which he swore to your ancestors, as it is today.
Realizing that God wants to give you the desires of your heart.

Covenant blessings of prosperity: spirit, soul and body including all people and animals in your sphere of influence

Fruit of the Spirit

God lives in us and we live in Him. Because we are in intimate relationship, as we pray, or worship or communicate with God, we are transformed from glory to glory into the image and likeness of Christ. The Holy Spirit on the inside teaches us through the word of God and as we believe the word of God, it produces in us, godly character.

Galatians 5: 22 But the fruit of the Spirit is love, joy, peace, forbearance, kindness, goodness, faithfulness, 23 gentleness and self-control. Against such things there is no law.

God Gives you the Desires of your Heart

It is God's desire to give us what pleases us. I am not talking about anything outside the will of God. I am not talking about carnal pleasures that are sinful. If we are living our lives wholly given to Christ, God wants to bless us and give us the desires of our hearts.

Psalm 37: 4 Take delight in the Lord,
   and he will give you the desires of your heart.

Luke 12: 32 "Do not be afraid, little flock, for your Father has been pleased to give you the kingdom.

Matthew 21: 22 If you believe, you will receive whatever you ask for in prayer."

John 14: 13 And I will do whatever you ask in my name, so that the Father may be glorified in the Son. 14 You may ask me for anything in my name, and I will do it.

An Important Part of the Body of Christ

Once we accept Christ, the Holy Spirit lives in us and we live in God. We become part of the Universal Body of Christ. That means we function as part of the Body of Christ and we are nourished by God's Word, preaching and teaching. It means we care about all the other parts of the Body.

1 Corinthians 12: 12 Just as a body, though one, has many parts, but all its many parts form one body, so it is with Christ.

1 Corinthians 12 27 Now you are the body of Christ, and each one of you is a part of it.:

Ministry

After we become Christians, God imparts to us the great commission; we are to share Christ with all people in our lives. God entrusts to us the message of reconciliation to God or how to get right with God.

2 Corinthians 5: 18 All this is from God, who reconciled us to himself through Christ and gave us the ministry of reconciliation: 19 that God was reconciling the world to himself in Christ, not counting people's sins against them. And he has committed to us the message of reconciliation. 20 We are therefore Christ's ambassadors, as though God were making his appeal through us. We implore you on Christ's behalf: Be reconciled to God. 21 God made him who had no sin to be sin[b] for us, so that in him we might become the righteousness of God.

1 Corinthians 3: 7 So neither the one who plants nor the one who waters is anything, but only God, who makes things grow. 8 The one who plants and the one who waters have one purpose, and they will each be rewarded according to their own labor. 9 For we are co-workers in God's service; you are God's field, God's building.

End of Chapter Questions

1. Write down the blessings you have personally experienced of being in the New Covenant with Jesus Christ. Share these with a family member or loved one, or post it to your Facebook page.
2. Explain to a family member or close friend what it means to be a member of the Body of Christ. Ask him or her to share his or her perspective.
3. Explain your role in the Body of Christ.

Conclusion

If you have read this book because you are interested in God and His covenants, I pray God may use you to use it to share with others, pointing to Jesus Christ our Saviour to anyone who will believe. If you have read this book because you want to know God, may God quicken Himself to you through the scriptures so that faith ignites your spirit to believe.

Salvation Prayer

O God, thank you for the covenants you have made with people throughout the years. I want what you offer me – eternal life. Thank you, Jesus that you died for my sins. Thank you that you rose from the dead and ascended into heaven. I believe and I receive salvation. Thank you for giving me good teachers and preachers and strong Christian friends so that I can become a strong Christian. I believe that you are my Saviour and I want you to be the LORD or head of my life. I give myself to you. Separate me unto yourself in Jesus name. Amen.

Disciple's Prayer

O God, thank you for quickening me by the refreshing of what you did through the convents you made with people throughout human history. God, I want the best that you have for me. I want the New Covenant to be so evident in my life that others come to know you. I want to live holy, set apart for you. Thank you for dying for my sins. Thank you for setting me free from sin and from the curse of sin. Thank you for healing. Thank you for prosperity. Thank you for long life. Use me to share the good news of Jesus Christ the Messiah with as many people as I can. I give my life to you fresh. Fill me. I give you all of me: spirit, soul and body as a living sacrifice. Amen.

OTHER BOOKS BY CHRIS A. LEGEBOW

Available on Amazon.ca Amazon.com or Amazon.ca or Kindle
Or the Create Space webstore.

Living Word Publishers

An Excellent Spirit: Living Life Wholly Unto God.

Covenant With God: God's Relationship With Man

Discovering and Using your Spiritual Gifts.

Kinds of Prayer. Knowing Them and Using Them Effectively:

Living Life Fully: Knowing your Purpose.

The Anointing: the Glory of God.

The High Calling: Life Worth Living.

ABOUT THE AUTHOR

Chris Legebow is a Christian Professor of English and Communications. She has taught at the elementary, high school and College and University levels. She has ministered in her local churches in intercessory prayer, teaching Sunday school and other Christian Doctrine classes to children and youths. She has preached to congregations and given her testimony. Although she was not raised in a Christian home, she came to know Jesus Christ as her Saviour and LORD while she was studying in University. This radically transformed her life in terms of priorities and commitment. She has a strong passion for the great commission – that Jesus Christ would be preached throughout all the earth believing that it a major sign of the LORD's return. She has been a part of several different types of full gospel charismatic churches but has also gained much of her insight and enlightenment from Christian Media and broadcasting. She hopes to continue ministering, serving, interceding and giving and teaching until the LORD returns.

Printed in Great Britain
by Amazon

35879869R00057